UNDERSTANDING THE CATECHISM

Liturgy and Sacraments

CHARLES CHESNAVAGE

RESOURCES FOR CHRISTIAN LIVING™
Allen, Texas

> "The Ad Hoc Committee to Oversee
> the Use of the Catechism,
> National Conference of Catholic Bishops,
> has found this catechetical text
> to be in conformity with
> the *Catechism of the Catholic Church*."

President: Kim Duty
Publisher: Maryann Nead
Catechetical Advisor: Jacquie Jambor
Editorial Director: Ed DeStefano

Author: Charles Chesnavage

Product Manager: Mike Carotta
Senior Editor: Ron Lamping
Project Editor: Karen Griffith
Senior Production Editor: Laura Fremder

Art Director: Pat Bracken
Page Design: Dennis Davidson
Production Manager: Jenna Nelson
Cover Design: Pat Bracken

NIHIL OBSTAT
Rev. Msgr. Glenn D. Gardner, J.C.D.
Censor Librorum

IMPRIMATUR
† Most Rev. Charles V. Grahmann
Bishop of Dallas

July 15, 1998

The Nihil Obstat and Imprimatur are official declarations
that the material reviewed is free of doctrinal or moral
error. No implication is contained therein that those
granting the Nihil Obstat and Imprimatur agree with
the contents, opinions, or statements expressed.

ACKNOWLEDGMENTS

Scripture selections are taken from the *New American
Bible* © 1991, 1986, 1970 by the Confraternity of
Christian Doctrine, Washington, D.C., and are used by
license of the copyright owner. All rights reserved. No
part of the New American Bible may be used or repro-
duced in any form, without the permission of the
copyright owner.

Excerpts from the English translation of the *Catechism
of the Catholic Church* for the United States of America
copyright © 1994 United States Catholic Conference,
Inc.—Libreria Editrice Vaticana. Used with permission.

Excerpts from *Vatican Council II: The Conciliar and
Post Conciliar Documents, New Revised Edition,* Austin
Flannery, O.P., Gen. Ed. Copyright © 1975, 1986, 1992,
1996 by Costello Publishing Company, Inc. Used by
permission.

Photos: L. Dematteis/The ImageWorks, 42; Nigel
Dickinson/Tony Stone Images, 92; Full Photographics,
11, 14, 22, 31, 46, 60, 65, 100, 111, 121; Paul A.
Hein/Unicorn Stock Photos, 80; Photofest, 68, 116; Bill
Wittman, 6.

Send all inquiries to:
RCL • Resources for Christian Living™
200 East Bethany Drive
Allen, Texas 75002-3804

Toll Free   800-822-6701
Fax   800-688-8356

Printed in the United States of America

20252   ISBN 0-7829-0874-8 (Student Workbook)
20253   ISBN 0-7829-0875-6 (Teacher's Guide)

1 2 3 4 5   02 01 00 99 98

Contents

Introduction

Welcome to this book on principles and foundations of the celebration of the Christian mystery, the liturgy and sacraments celebrated by the Catholic Church. It derives its inspiration from the *Catechism of the Catholic Church* (CCC), which was published in October 1992. The *Catechism* presents the essential teachings of our Catholic faith authoritatively, systematically, and comprehensively.

The source of the teachings of our Catholic faith is Sacred Scripture and Sacred Tradition, both of which pass on to us divine Revelation. Our official church teachers, which we call the Magisterium of the Church, authentically interpret and pass this revelation on to us.

The *Catechism* is a remarkable resource book for all Catholics. It is divided into four main parts. The four parts have come to be called the four pillars, or foundations, of the *Catechism*. They are:

❑ The Profession of Faith
  (The Creed)
❑ The Celebration of the Christian
  Mystery
  (Worship: Liturgy and Sacraments)
❑ Life in Christ
  (Moral Living)
❑ Christian Prayer

The *Catechism* is more than seven hundred pages in its English translation. As a result, the *Catechism* itself encourages us to adapt it. This book, *Understanding the Catechism: Liturgy and Sacraments,* is one part of a four-book series on the *Catechism*. This series has been especially written for Catholic high school students.

Understanding the Catechism: Liturgy and Sacraments will introduce you to the major content of the second part of the *Catechism*—The Celebration of the Christian Mystery. It will introduce you to or review for you the teachings of the Church that guide us in celebrating our life in Christ.

[B]e filled with the Spirit, addressing one another [in] psalms and hymns and spiritual songs, singing and playing to the Lord in your hearts, giving thanks always and for everything in the name of our Lord Jesus Christ to God the Father.

Ephesians 5:18–20

CHAPTER 1

Seasons of Love, Life, and Faith

There is an appointed time for everything,
and a time for every affair under the heavens.

ECCLESIASTES 3:1

What Do You Think?

In the space provided, write "A" if you agree with the statement, "D" if you disagree with it, or "N" if you have no opinion about it.

_____ 1. Christmas and Easter are two seasons of the liturgical year.

_____ 2. Lent celebrates the resurrection of Jesus.

_____ 3. Easter takes place in the winter.

_____ 4. The liturgical seasons teach us about the life, death, and resurrection of Jesus.

_____ 5. The Jewish feast of Passover celebrates the resurrection of Jesus.

Leo Buscaglia's book *The Fall of Freddie the Leaf* is "a story of life for all ages." In it Freddie is a leaf on a tree with many other leaves. He has many friends on the tree; but his favorite is Daniel, the wisest leaf. Wondering about the changes the tree undergoes as the seasons change from spring to summer, fall, and winter, Freddie asks Daniel, "What's a purpose? Will we all die? Does the tree die, too? Where will we go when we die? Will we return in the spring? Then what has been the reason for all of this? Why were we here at all if we only have to fall and die?"

Daniel answers Freddie's final questions about purpose and reason for living in a matter-of-fact way: "It's been about the sun and the moon. It's been about happy times together. It's been about the shade and old people and the children. It's been about seasons. Isn't that enough?"

Many of the questions that Freddie asks are questions human beings have asked themselves over the centuries. They are certainly questions that we face during our encounters with God, religion, and our own life experience.

If you were Daniel, the wisest leaf on the tree, how would you answer Freddie's questions?

KEY TERMS

Advent

Christmas

Easter

Incarnation

Lent

Ordinary Time

Pentecost

Triduum

What do the natural seasons teach us about life? About ourselves? About God? If we don't take the seasons of the year for granted, they teach us much about the continual cycle of life and death, happiness and sadness, the value and need for change—and many other insights into life. The Church's year also has a rhythm marked by seasons. In this chapter we will explore the seasons of the Church's liturgical year.

(*Catechism of the Catholic Church,* 524–525, 638–640, 654, 1095, 1163–1165, 1168–1171, 1173, 1363–1364)

The Liturgical Cycle of the Church

The liturgical cycle of the Church's year recalls for us and celebrates the life, death, and resurrection of Jesus through the specific seasons of **Advent, Christmas, Ordinary Time, Lent,** and **Easter.**

Advent

Advent is a word that means "something is coming." It is also the root of *adventure,* which refers to "an exciting undertaking and experience, with potential surprises." The liturgical cycle begins in late November or early December with the first Sunday of Advent and proceeds for four Sundays leading up to Christmas. Advent is a time of preparation for both the first and the second coming of Jesus. The First Coming refers to the birth of Jesus, celebrated on December 25. The Second (or Final) Coming refers to Jesus' return at the end of time, otherwise known as the Parousia.

For Reflection
● ● ● ● ● ● ● ● ● ● ● ● ● ● ● ●

Just as the seasons taught Freddie, they can teach us many things about life, too.

Take some time and write out what you like and dislike about each of the natural seasons: winter, spring, summer, and fall.

What does each season tell you about human life? Why?

What does each season tell you about the political arena?

Unfortunately in our American culture, the Christmas season begins after Halloween and ends, for many people, the day after Christmas. This creates a challenge for us, since Advent is meant to be a subdued time of preparation— not at all like the spirit of commercialism that is typical of our culture.

The beginning of the season of Advent is filled with references to the Second Coming at the end of time. These are sobering warnings about Judgment Day. But, for the faithful Christian, the Second Coming is a day of vindication and reward. The earliest believers cried out, "Maranatha"—a cry of joyful expectation and anticipation that means "Come, Lord Jesus!" It is with this spirit of joyful expectation and anticipation that we are invited to begin our celebration of the season of Advent. As Christmas approaches, the focus of Advent shifts from the Second Coming to the First Coming, the birth of the Son of God in human flesh. Our watchfulness for his advent is meant to grow ever greater.

Christmas

Although Christmas has become highly commercialized, it is one of the most popular and widely celebrated liturgical seasons of the Church's year. Unfortunately, in our culture Christmas is over as soon as it arrives. But this is not the case in the Church's celebration of Christmas.

Christmas begins with the Vigil Mass on December 24 and continues until the feast of the Baptism of the Lord. This season is filled with special feasts, which include:

❏ Saint Stephen, the first martyr (December 26)

❏ Saint John, Apostle and Evangelist (December 27)

❏ Holy Innocents, Martyrs (December 28)

❏ Holy Family Sunday

❏ Mary, the Mother of God (January 1)

❏ Epiphany

❏ Baptism of the Lord

During Advent we hear passages like "Be watchful! Be alert! You do not know when the time will come. . . . What I say to you, I say to all: 'Watch!' " (Mark 13:33, 37). These passages, obviously, speak to the Second Coming at the end of time. Jesus reminds us, "You cannot know the day your Lord is coming!" "The Son of Man is coming at the time you least expect."

Read and reflect on Matthew 25:31–46. Two groups of people, the sheep and the goats, are judged by their actions toward people in need. Fill in the blanks with actions for today's problems and describe how our actions can help others.

PROBLEM   **ACTIONS**

Hunger _____

Thirst _____

Immigration _____

Homelessness _____

Suffering and illness _____

Imprisonment _____

. . . . Discuss:
How might these actions mark the coming of God among people?

It takes several weeks for the Church to celebrate the birth of Jesus, fulfilling Isaiah's prophecy of the coming of Emmanuel (Isaiah 7:14, Matthew 1:23), a name meaning "God with us."

Infancy Narratives. Did you know that there are two Christmas stories, or infancy narratives, in the Gospels that describe the birth of Jesus? Each is unique and different.

Matthew's infancy narrative (Matthew 1–2) includes the visit of the Magi, or wise men, from the East, following the star to the city of Bethlehem and bearing gifts for Jesus. The Magi represent all the nations of the world, acknowledging Jesus to be the Savior of the world. After paying homage to Jesus, the Magi did not return and report their visit to Herod, who deceitfully told them that he also wanted to pay homage to the newborn "Messiah" of Israel.

Later, Herod, in a rage, ordered the death of all boys under age two in the city of Bethlehem. The Holy Family of Jesus, Mary, and Joseph then fled into Egypt, where they remained until it was safe to return.

Luke's infancy narrative (Luke 1:5–2:52) includes Jesus being born in a manger, because there was no room in the inn. The angels announce the birth to the shepherds, the poorest people in town. They were the first to hear the good news of the birth of the Savior, who is Messiah and Lord. After visiting the manger, they spread the word about what they had learned and seen.

The heart of the Christmas season is our belief that the child born to Mary in Bethlehem truly was the Son of God, fully divine and fully human. The word

Christmas in the Movies

The meaning of the Nativity has often been portrayed in the media, especially in movies and on television. What lessons can we learn from such Christmas films as *It's a Wonderful Life, A Christmas Carol, The Grinch Who Stole Christmas,* and *Rudolph the Red-Nosed Reindeer?*

Choose one of the above or another movie about Christmas and describe the ways it portrays the true meaning of Christmas and the ways it might mistakenly represent Christmas.

Title: _____

True Meaning

Mistaken Meaning

The Christmas creche. Christians traditionally set up a creche in the home and churches. The origins of the creche date to Saint Francis of Assisi (1181–1226), who tradition says first used the creche.

incarnation is the term used to name this miraculous union of a divine and a human nature in one person, Jesus.

Our faith recognizes that because of the Incarnation, everything about the person of Jesus has special significance. He is called "Savior" because his life has special meaning as God's Son. Christmas is such an important feast in the liturgical cycle because it marks the birth of our salvation.

Ordinary Time

Ordinary Time focuses on the overall life of Jesus. It is the longest season of the liturgical year. It takes place at two different times of the year. Beginning after the Christmas season (that is, the Sunday after the Baptism of the Lord), the first part of Ordinary Time goes until Ash Wednesday, which begins the season of Lent. The second (and longest) part of Ordinary Time resumes on the day after **Pentecost** Sunday

(that is, after the seasons of Lent and Easter are over). It continues until Advent begins the liturgical cycle over again.

The season of Ordinary Time helps us recognize that something extraordinary is happening in the ordinary happenings of our own life. For example, waking up in the morning can be a simple, ordinary event. Waking up, however, can be valued as another opportunity to live our life with God. When we begin to see each ordinary event as an "extraordinary opportunity" to make a difference or offer thanks to God, we begin to understand the meaning of Ordinary Time. It is not so ordinary after all.

During Ordinary Time the gospel readings at Sunday Mass follow in sequence the story of Jesus' public ministry. In that way Ordinary Time is also an invitation to us to walk with Jesus as his followers. It is an extraordinary opportunity for us to learn what it means to be his disciples.

Lent

Lent is the special season that begins on Ash Wednesday and ends with the Mass of the Lord's Supper on Holy Thursday. The celebration of Lent begins with our receiving ashes with the words, "Turn away from sin and be faithful to the gospel" *(Roman Missal)*.

Ashes are a symbol of death and repentance. Having ashes placed on our foreheads for all to see reminds us to think about how we are living our life in Christ. During Lent we pray, fast, and share what we have with others, especially those in need. Such Lenten activities help strengthen our relationship with God and with one another.

The first Sunday of Lent, which is the Sunday after Ash Wednesday, always recounts the temptation of Jesus in the desert, when he was tempted three times by Satan. The temptations Jesus faced are three basic temptations every person faces: the temptations to seek pleasure, power, and popularity in place of God.

The meaning of the Lenten season is found in the name given to this period of time in the Rite of Christian Initiation of Adults: The Period of Purification and Enlightenment. Lent is a time of final purification, a kind of retreat, for those who will be baptized at the Easter Vigil.

During the Lenten season, the whole Church is asked to take part in the process of repentance and to join in solidarity with those to be baptized. We are to be purified by turning away from our sins. This is why so many Christians do penance and celebrate the sacrament of Reconciliation during Lent.

Those to be baptized are also being enlightened by their growing faith in Jesus. And so Lent has a very positive emphasis on the many ways that our eyes are opened to see Jesus as our Lord and Savior.

The climax of the season of Lent for the catechumens (those to be baptized) is their initiation celebrated in the three Sacraments of Initiation—Baptism, Confirmation, and the Eucharist. The climax of the season of Lent for the rest of the church community happens in the Masses of Easter, when we renew our own initiation by making the baptismal promises and being sprinkled with the Easter water. It is for this that Lent is meant to prepare us.

During Lent we are called to fast, pray, and give alms to those in need as ways to be purified and enlightened. It is a time to be changed by the saving grace of God and to renew our baptismal commitment to be authentic followers of Jesus.

Easter Triduum

The term **triduum** means "three days." It refers to Holy Thursday, Good Friday, and Holy Saturday—the three special days of Holy Week that precede Easter. It is important to know what each of these days celebrates.

Holy Thursday. On Holy Thursday, with the celebration of the Evening Mass of the Lord's Supper, the Church commemorates the night before Jesus died, when he had his last supper with his disciples. We remember his breaking the bread and sharing the cup of wine, which he gave as his body and blood, the food and drink. They become for us sign and symbol of the New

What the Documents Say

....

This instruction is given in the Rite of Christian Initiation of Adults.

> (Lent) is a time for spiritual recollection in preparation for the celebration of the paschal mystery.
> *Rite of Christian Initiation of Adults,* 138

Brainstorm a plan of action that young people could follow to take part more fully in the Lenten season.

Covenant that Jesus established with his people, fulfilled in his saving death and resurrection.

It is also the night Jesus stooped to wash the feet of his disciples, giving us an example of humble service that we are meant to imitate. The liturgy of Holy Thursday celebrates the mystery of the Eucharist, the institution of the priesthood, and Jesus' commandment of love.

Good Friday. The Church gathers and celebrates the liturgy of the celebration of the Lord's Passion on Good Friday. The liturgy of Good Friday includes the Liturgy of the Word, which concludes with solemn prayers of intercession for the Church and the world, an invitation for all present to venerate the cross of Jesus, and the sharing in Holy Communion.

During the Liturgy of the Word, the Passion according to John is read. We recall the suffering and death of Jesus through the terrible torture of crucifixion. He was charged as a criminal, found guilty though innocent, and executed by the death penalty of his day. A sign above his head mocked him as "the King of the Jews."

Is death something we always need to fear, or does our faith in the death and resurrection of Jesus allow us to see death differently? The death of Jesus opened the door to eternal life through which all who believe in him are promised eternal life.

It is because of the death of Jesus on Good Friday that every Friday is meant to be a day of fasting and prayer throughout the year, but especially during Lent.

Holy Saturday. This, for the most part, is a quiet day of preparation and continued fasting and prayer as we keep vigil while Jesus lies in the tomb. The celebration of the Easter Vigil later this night begins Easter proper with its fifty days of feasting, after forty days of fasting. The celebration of Christ's resurrection at the vigil service is the most solemn and most dramatic liturgy of the Church's year. We have been given a vision for our life on earth. Jesus' resurrection from death destroyed death's power over us.

At the beginning of the Easter Vigil, a fire is lighted in a darkened church.

The Paschal candle is lighted from the fire and carried into the church in procession, representing the Risen Christ, who brings light and life to the darkness of death. The stories of our salvation are then read from numerous places in both the Old Testament and the New Testament. After the lengthy Liturgy of the Word, Christ's resurrection is *experienced* in the faithful's renewal of their baptismal promises and in the celebration of the Sacraments of Initiation. New members of the Body of Christ are baptized, confirmed, and share in the Eucharist for the first time.

The blessing of the fire and lighting of the candle at the Easter Vigil.

Easter

Easter is a word that points to the direction of the east. It is in the east that the sun rises every morning, and it was on a Sunday *morning* that the women disciples found the tomb empty. The risen Jesus would later appear to his disciples and others over a period of forty days. Before ascending to his Father in heaven, he promised his disciples that he would be with them forever and commissioned them to "go, therefore, and make disciples of all nations, baptizing them in the name of the Father, and of the Son, and of the holy Spirit" (Matthew 28:19).

Pentecost is the fiftieth—and final—day of the Easter season. This feast celebrates the descent of the Holy Spirit upon the disciples, filling them with the fire to preach God's saving message of faith, hope, and love to the world.

Because Jesus rose from the dead on the Sunday after his death and burial, Sunday has become known as the Lord's Day. It is the principal day for the celebration of the Eucharist. Sunday is the "pre-eminent day of the liturgical assembly, the day of the Christian family, and the day of joy and rest from work. Sunday is 'the foundation and kernel of the whole liturgical year' (*Constitution on the Sacred Liturgy,* 106)" (CCC, 1193). Saint Jerome writes:

> The Lord's day, the day of Resurrection, the day of Christians, is our day. It is called the Lord's day because on it the Lord rose victorious to the Father. *On Easter*

Feasts of the Church

❖ ❖ ❖

On certain days of the liturgical year the Church honors Mary, the Mother of God, and the apostles, martyrs, and other saints because of their example of being faithful followers of Jesus. We join our prayers to theirs to give worship and praise to the Father, Son, and Holy Spirit.

Look up and name some of the major feasts celebrated by the Church. In what ways does each celebrate the faith of the church community?

IMPORTANT TERMS TO KNOW

Advent—a word meaning "something is coming"; the four-week liturgical season of preparation for and expectation of Christmas

Christmas—the liturgical season that celebrates the birth of Jesus; it begins December 24 and lasts until the feast of the Baptism of the Lord.

Easter—the liturgical season that celebrates Jesus' resurrection, ascension to his Father in heaven, and the gift of the Holy Spirit to the Church

Incarnation—the term used to name the miraculous union of a divine and a human nature in one person, Jesus

Lent—the liturgical season that prepares catechumens and the whole Church to celebrate Christ's resurrection at Easter, especially in the sacraments of Baptism, Confirmation, and the Eucharist

Ordinary Time—the time of the liturgical cycle that celebrates in general the public life and ministry of Jesus; it takes place at two times during the year—between Christmas and Lent, and between Easter and Advent.

Pentecost—the fiftieth—and last—day of the Easter season that celebrates the descent of the Holy Spirit upon the disciples in the upper room

Triduum—the three holy days that precede Easter: Holy Thursday, Good Friday, and Holy Saturday

CHAPTER SUMMARY

The natural seasons of the year teach us much about the cycle of life, death, and rebirth. In this chapter we explored the liturgical seasons of the Church's year and how they help us celebrate and enter into the life, death, and resurrection of Christ.

1. The liturgical seasons are Advent, Christmas, Ordinary Time, Lent, and Easter.

2. Advent is a four-week period of celebrating both the first and the second coming of Jesus. Christmas celebrates the birth of Jesus and includes feasts that remember the martyrdom of Stephen, the Holy Family, the slaughter of the Holy Innocents, the motherhood of Mary, the visit of the Magi (Epiphany), and the Baptism of the Lord.

3. Lent is a forty-day period of prayer, fasting, and almsgiving. During this time the catechumens prepare for Baptism, and the rest of the Church, in solidarity with the catechumens, prepares to renew its baptismal commitment. The Triduum is the center of the liturgical year. It celebrates in a dramatic way the Paschal mystery of Christ.

4. Easter celebrates the resurrection of Jesus Christ from the dead. The season is fifty days long and ends with Pentecost Sunday.

5. Ordinary Time remembers the events in the public life and ministry of Jesus. It is the longest season of the Church's year.

6. Sunday is the Lord's Day. It is a day we are called to gather as a community of faith to hear God's Word and celebrate the Eucharist.

7. On some days Mary, the Mother of God, and the apostles, martyrs, and saints are honored and remembered as examples of faith.

EXPLORING OUR CATHOLIC FAITH

1. Listening to God's Word

Paul reminds us that "we walk by faith, not by sight" (2 Corinthians 5:7). How does this teaching help us take part in the celebration of the liturgical year of the Church?

2. Understanding the Teachings of the Catholic Church

The bishops of the Second Vatican Council taught: "In the course of the year, moreover, [the Church] unfolds the whole mystery of Christ from the incarnation and nativity to the ascension, to Pentecost and the expectation of the blessed hope of the coming of the Lord" (*Constitution on the Sacred Liturgy*, 102). Using what was presented in this chapter, explain that teaching in more detail.

3. Reflecting on Our Catholic Faith

Saint Athanasius (c. A.D. 297–373) has called Easter the "Great Sunday." How does this insight help you take part in the Sunday celebration of the Eucharist? Write your thoughts in your journal.

4. Living Our Catholic Faith

Brainstorm ways we can celebrate Sunday as the Lord's Day.

CHAPTER 2

A Holy People, a Holy Place

Come to him, a living stone.

1 PETER 2:4

What Do You Think?

Imagine you are in your parish church. In this space list the images that come to your mind.

In 1206, after his conversion, Saint Francis of Assisi was just beginning his new life as a servant of God. One day he entered an old abandoned church half in ruins in San Damiano, outside of Assisi, Italy. While kneeling in prayer, Francis looked up at a crucifix that hung above the altar. He heard Christ speaking, "Francis, go and restore my house, which, as you see, is going to ruin."

Francis took the message literally, and began to rebuild the church of San Damiano. But there was a deeper meaning to the message. God was calling Francis to give up all that he had, follow Jesus, and serve the poorest of the poor. Francis was called to rebuild, or bring new life into, the Church, the People of God.

We too have a vocation to rebuild the Church for the next generation of believers. We are called to pass on our traditions and the teachings of the Gospel to present and future generations. What ideas do you have about "rebuilding" the Church of today and the Church of tomorrow?

San Damiano at Assisi. The first church to be restored by Francis.

Francis brought new life to the Church, the People of God. His love for Christ and the Church continues to attract and motivate men and women to dedicate their lives to continue his work. Francis reached out to people just as Jesus did. He called them to praise and bless God for the gift of his love revealed to us in so many ways, especially in the Paschal mystery of Jesus' suffering-death-resurrection.

Francis was a living stone that built up the Church. In this chapter we will explore the mystery of the Church as both the worshiping assembly gathered to bless and praise God and the place, or building, in which the assembly gathers.

This meaning of liturgy helps us understand the role of the *entire assembly* upon entering a church to worship and give thanks and praise to God *publicly*. It is in the gathered assembly of the faithful that the Real Presence of Jesus is known.

In Paul's letter to the Ephesians he gives them this advice:

> [B]e filled with the Spirit, addressing one another [in] psalms and hymns and spiritual songs, singing and playing to the Lord in your hearts, giving thanks always and for everything in the name of our Lord Jesus Christ to God the Father.
>
> **Ephesians 5:18–20**

This is a perfect example of full, active, conscious participation in the early Church.

Listen to how Saint Augustine of Hippo (A.D. 354–430), the great African saint, describes his experience while participating in the liturgy:

> How I wept, deeply moved by your hymns, songs, and the voices that echoed through your Church! What emotion I experienced in them! Those sounds flowed into my ears, distilling the truth in my heart. A feeling of devotion surged within me, and tears streamed down my face—tears that did me good.
>
> *Confessions,* 9, 6, 14

It is no surprise that this same Augustine is famous for his quote, "He who sings prays twice!"

(*Catechism of the Catholic Church,* 1136, 1140–1144)

The Worshiping Assembly

The word **liturgy** is from the Greek word meaning "work of the people." It is the whole *community,* the Body of Christ united with its Head, that celebrates.

> Liturgical services are not private functions but are celebrations of the Church which is "the sacrament of unity," namely, the holy people united and organized under the authority of the bishops.
>
> *Constitution on the Sacred Liturgy,* 26

The Church teaches that all members of the worshiping assembly are to take a full, conscious, and active part in the liturgy. When you are part of a liturgy, do you feel you are fully, consciously, and actively participating in the celebration? Or do you feel more like a passive observer, bored with the whole thing? Why do you think you feel the way you do?

What does full, conscious, and active participation mean? Do you think most people understand this to be their role upon entering a church for liturgy? Give reasons for your responses.

Presider

The worshiping assembly is led, or presided over, by the presider, or celebrant. At the celebration of the Eucharist, it is the priest who presides over the celebration. As the leader of prayer and as the "icon" of Christ, he sets the tone of the Eucharist with his welcoming remarks and his prayerful spirit. He prays the great prayer of thanksgiving, the eucharistic prayer, on behalf of those gathered with him. However, the priest is not the only person who presides at liturgical celebrations. The deacon can preside at baptisms, weddings, and funerals. Non-ordained laypeople can lead the congregation in Communion services and other types of prayer services.

Ministers of the Word

Much emphasis is placed on the proclamation of the Word of God and on the ministers of the Word who proclaim it. From the opening procession, when all of the ministers proceed toward the altar, the Lectionary is held high for all to see. Sometimes incense is part of the procession and sometimes it is used before the reading of the Gospel. All of these actions remind us, through seeing and smelling the special fragrance, that the proclamation of God's Word is a powerful event.

Deacon proclaiming the Gospel.

A reader is needed to proclaim God's Word clearly and articulately for all to hear. We respond with several different acclamations:

❏ "Thanks be to God!"

❏ "Glory to you, O Lord!"(as we mark our forehead, lips, and heart with the sign of the cross, reminding us that the Lord is in our heart and on our lips)

❏ "Praise to you, Lord Jesus Christ!"

We also sing the psalm response.

Finally, the deacon, priest, or bishop who gives the homily after the proclamation of the Gospel nourishes the gathered assembly by strengthening us with the meaning of God's Word and God's love for today's world. At the conclusion of the liturgy, he charges the assembly to live out this message, saying:

> Go in peace to love and
> serve the Lord.

Ministers of Music/ Leaders of Song

The choir, the cantor, the organist, the musicians, and the gathered assembly all contribute with their music to the community's prayer. We know that the music we use in the celebration of the liturgy is doing its work correctly when it adds to our prayer, when it helps the assembly to experience a unity in their participation, and when it adds reverence to the celebration.

Ministers of the Altar

The altar servers, boys and girls, assist the priest on the altar. They lend a prayerful presence to the proceedings and should be role models of full, conscious, and active participation.

Ministers of the Eucharist

Eucharistic ministers assist the priest at the time of distribution of Holy Communion. They share the Body and Blood of Christ by offering the bread and wine to the faithful. Their ministry is also to take Holy Communion to those who are sick or homebound after the Eucharist is celebrated.

Reflection

Various forms of Christian piety, which are often rooted in different cultures, also give expression to our faith. These practices of Christian piety, connected with our participation in the liturgy, nourish and strengthen our Christian life.

.... Discuss:

What practices of Christian piety enrich your parish's life? Your own Christian life? How do they express your faith? How do they nourish your life in Christ?

Church

The Second Vatican Council taught at great length that the Church is the new People of God.

.... Discuss:

Compare the church as a gathering place to the Church as the People of God.

(CCC, 1179–1186)

The Place of Worship and Prayer

The church is a place where the People of God called by Christ come together to celebrate and be nourished. It is a place "that invites us to the

recollection and silent prayer that extend and internalize the great prayer of the Eucharist" (CCC, 1185).

The physical environment of our churches contains certain key elements. These include the altar, the ambo, the presider's chair, and the baptistry.

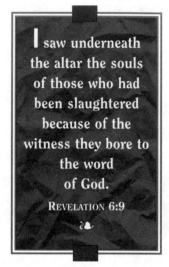

I saw underneath the altar the souls of those who had been slaughtered because of the witness they bore to the word of God.

REVELATION 6:9

Altar

The central, most obvious part of the church is the **altar.** It is around the altar that the faithful gather as the Body of Christ to celebrate the Eucharist and to share the "Bread of Life."

Some altars have grains of wheat and grapes embedded or carved into the front. These symbols remind us of the bread and wine that become the Body and Blood of Jesus.

The altar is also a symbol of Christ's presence. For this reason the priest kisses the altar at the beginning of the Eucharist. It is anointed with the scented chrism oil by marking five crosses on it, one on each corner and one in the center.

Ambo

Near the altar you will see the **ambo,** the place where the Word of God is proclaimed. Some ambos are very simple and plain in design. Others are more ornate. Oftentimes the ambo will match the altar in some way or have symbols built into it. For example, images representing the four evangelists are sometimes part of the design of the ambo—an eagle for John, an ox for Luke, a lion for Mark, and an angel for Matthew.

No matter how the ambo is designed and decorated, it is here that the Word of God is to be proclaimed with conviction and authority. Saint Augustine of Hippo spoke of the ambo as the table of God's Word that nourishes us, just as the table of the Eucharist feeds us on the Body and Blood of Christ.

Presider's Chair

The presider's chair stands as a symbol of the priest's office of presiding over the assembly and of leading worship. In a cathedral the presider's chair is called the **cathedra** and only the bishop sits there when he presides. The presider's chair is usually located in a place in the sanctuary where the presider can have the best communication with everyone gathered for prayer and worship.

Baptistry

The **baptistry** is the place where infants, children, and adults are baptized. It is here that the baptismal font, which can be a large, elevated bowl or a deep pool for people to step into, is located. Like the altar and the

The Way of Jesus

Many other symbols can be found in our churches.

❏ Stations of the Cross usually surround the entire area of the assembly. Each station represents a part of the journey Jesus traveled when he carried his cross to his death.

❏ Stained-glass windows will usually tell many Bible stories or portray something about the personality of the parish and its history.

❏ Statues, mosaics, and paintings of Jesus; his mother, Mary; or saints may decorate a church and add to its personality.

List as many such symbols as you can that are found in your parish church. Share how they lead you closer to Jesus.

ambo, the baptistry often has symbols built into it that remind us of the meaning of the sacrament of Baptism. Symbols often used include John the Baptist baptizing Jesus, a fish, an ark, or other baptismal symbols.

The baptistry is located in various places in the church. In some churches it is found at the entrance of the church; in others, near the altar; in still others, it is in a chapel located in the back or on the side of the church.

Other Elements of the Physical Environment of Our Churches

In addition to the central altar, the ambo, the presider's chair, and the baptistry, other elements included in our churches are the place of reposition of the Blessed Sacrament, which includes the tabernacle and the tabernacle light; the sacred, or holy, oils and the ambry; and the confessional or reconciliation chapel. Catholic churches also contain the Stations of the Cross, which help us remember and prayerfully reflect on and journey with Christ on the way of his Paschal mystery.

Tabernacle. The **tabernacle** is another very important part of our churches. It is here that the **Blessed Sacrament,** or consecrated bread (hosts), is stored for those who are sick and for the prayer and devotion of the people. People show their respect for the Real Presence of Jesus in the tabernacle by genuflecting, or bowing, in front of it. The tabernacle is to be situated " 'in churches in a most worthy place with the greatest honor' " (Paul VI, *The Mystery of Faith*).

One symbol often found on a tabernacle is the pelican piercing its side to feed its blood to its young babies. The legend this symbol portrays reminds us that the blood of Jesus saved us, and that his Body and Blood in the Eucharist feeds us in a spiritual way. The top of the tabernacle is sometimes shaped like a crown, reminding us of the kingship of Jesus and his royal presence.

> The beauty of the images moves me to contemplation, as a meadow delights the eyes and subtly infuses the soul with the glory of God.
>
> SAINT JOHN DAMASCENE

Tabernacle Light. One way to locate the tabernacle is to look for the burning tabernacle light, or sanctuary lamp. This is a sign that Jesus is truly present in the tabernacle in the form of the eucharistic bread.

Holy, or Sacred, Oils. Near the baptistry are the **holy oils.** These include the oil of catechumens, which is used with those preparing for the sacrament of Baptism; the oil of the sick, which is used in the sacrament of the Anointing of the Sick; and the sacred chrism, which is the scented oil used to consecrate a person in the sacraments of Baptism, Confirmation, and Holy Orders, or a sacred place, such as the altar. The place where the holy oils is kept is called the **ambry.**

Chapel of Reconciliation. The place in our churches where people go to celebrate God's love and forgiveness in the sacrament of Penance is called the confessional or the reconciliation chapel. In older churches, confessionals were dark places. Newer churches often have a reconciliation chapel with a brightly lighted room. The room usually has two chairs not separated by a screen, and a kneeler and a chair separated by a screen. This gives the person the choice of either facing the priest or not.

READING THE BIBLE

Prayerfully read and reflect on these gospel stories about what Jesus did in the Temple. Write down the differences in each of the stories.

Matthew 21:12–17

Mark 11:15–19

Luke 19:45–48

John 2:13–17

.... Discuss:

What is the central message of each of these gospel passages? What do they reveal about the deeper meaning of "what" our church buildings are?

Prayer

❖ ❖ ❖

Saint Francis of Assisi rebuilt the Church with concrete and living stones. Take the time to pray this famous prayer which captures the spirit of Saint Francis. Allow the words to lead and guide you to take action.

PRAYER OF SAINT FRANCIS

Lord, make me an instrument
of thy peace.
Where there is hatred let me
sow love;
Where there is injury, pardon;
Where there is doubt, faith;
Where there is despair, hope;
Where there is darkness, light;
Where there is sadness, joy.

O divine master, grant that I
may not so much seek
to be consoled as to console;
to be understood as to
understand;
To be loved as to love:
For it is in giving that we
receive;
It is in pardoning that we are
pardoned;
It is in dying that we are born
to eternal life.

IMPORTANT TERMS TO KNOW

altar—the table around which the Liturgy of the Eucharist is celebrated

ambo—the place where the Word of God is proclaimed

ambry—the place where the holy oils are kept

baptistry—the place where infants, children, and adults are baptized

Blessed Sacrament—another name given to the consecrated bread and wine, the Body and Blood of Jesus

cathedra—the chair in a cathedral where the bishop sits when leading, or presiding, at the liturgy

holy oils—the three sacred oils used in the liturgy: oil of the sick, oil of catechumens, and sacred chrism

liturgy—a Greek word that means "work of the people"; it refers to a gathering of the Christian community for prayer.

tabernacle—the place where the consecrated hosts are kept for those who are sick and for the prayer and devotion of the people

CHAPTER SUMMARY

A church is more than a building. It is the living stones that make up the Body of Christ alive in our world. In this chapter we looked at the Church—the worshiping assembly—and the parish church—the physical space in which the faithful gather for worship, prayer, and sharing the Word of God.

1. *Liturgy* is the Greek word that means "work of the people." It reminds us that we are to participate fully, actively, and consciously in the action, or work, of the Church at prayer.

2. The assembly celebrates the liturgy and is called to full, conscious, and active participation of the celebration.

3. The members of the worshiping assembly each have various roles. These roles are fulfilled by the presider, ministers of the Word, ministers of music, and ministers of the Eucharist.

4. The key elements or symbols of the physical environment of Catholic churches include the altar, the ambo, and the presider's chair (or in a cathedral, the cathedra).

5. Other key elements include the baptistry; the ambry; the place of reposition of the Blessed Sacrament, which includes the tabernacle and the tabernacle light; and the confessional or the reconciliation chapel.

EXPLORING OUR CATHOLIC FAITH

1. Listening to God's Word

Invite the Spirit's help and prayerfully read and reflect on the Word of God in Matthew 18:20: "[W]here two or three are gathered together in my name, there am I in the midst of them." What does this Scripture passage tell us about who we are and what we are called to be?

2. Understanding the Teachings of the Catholic Church

Visit your local church and describe, in detail, the parts of the church environment discussed in this chapter. Include as many details as possible regarding shape, pictures, and symbols on the various objects. Explain how they help the People of God worship.

3. Reflecting on Our Catholic Faith

Reflect on these words that give us insight into who we are and why we gather as the assembly of God's people: "What words can adequately describe God's gifts? They are so numerous that they defy enumeration. They are so great that any one of them demands our total gratitude in response" (Saint Basil the Great). Write your thoughts in your journal.

4. Living Our Catholic Faith

Design or compose your own "welcome announcement" inviting teenagers to your parish church.

CHAPTER 3

Symbols, Sacraments, and the Paschal Mystery

"You made them a kingdom and priests for our God, and they will reign on earth."

REVELATION 5:10

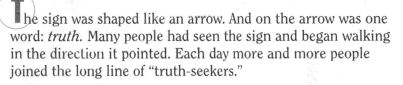

What Do You Think?

Share your reasons for agreeing or disagreeing with this statement:

Symbols have more than one meaning.

The sign was shaped like an arrow. And on the arrow was one word: *truth*. Many people had seen the sign and began walking in the direction it pointed. Each day more and more people joined the long line of "truth-seekers."

One day a traveler came by, saw the sign, and proceeded to pull it out of the ground. He happily walked away, knowing that he now had the truth all to himself. His search was over, while the others continued their search for the truth.

In this story a sign seems to be interpreted two different ways. Both the traveler and the "seekers" interpreted the sign in a literal way. The seekers walked in the direction toward which the sign pointed. The traveler was happy having the truth (or sign) in his personal possession.

Where is the truth in this story? What is the truth shared in this story?

KEY TERMS

anamnesis

catechesis

epiclesis

ex opere operato

lex orandi,
lex credendi

sacraments

World Youth Day, Denver, Colorado, 1993. Pope John Paul II joined with Catholic youth from around the world to celebrate the faith and its relevance to their lives.

Some signs have only one meaning. Mathematicians, for example, have agreed that + means only one thing. Symbols, however, always mean more than one thing. The color red, for example, depending on how it is used, can symbolize fire, love, anger, blood, and so on. A sign becomes a symbol when more than one meaning is associated with it.

(Catechism of the Catholic Church, 1145–1152)

Signs and Symbols

It should come as no surprise that religious people seeking the truth about God came to the earliest understanding about God by reflecting on the signs and wonders of nature. In ancient religions some elements of nature were even "deified," or worshiped as a god. There was the god of light, the god of darkness, the god of storms, and the god of wind.

Natural Signs

Signs and symbols in the natural world can reveal to us the existence of God and give us a glimpse of who God is. Signs in the human world can also teach us about our relationship with God.

Communication between humans is characterized by signs and symbols— by language, gestures, and actions. These have become part of our way of communicating with God as well. Walk into any church on a Sunday morning and quietly observe what is taking place. You will see people of all cultures communicating with God in their native languages; you will see people using such gestures as kneeling, sitting, and standing; you will see people speaking, singing, and using other symbolic actions that express their relationship with God.

Just as our ways of communicating with one another can take on a religious meaning, symbolic actions taken from our social life also can take on religious meaning. Washing, anointing, breaking bread, eating, sharing the cup, and drinking all take on a deeper meaning when they are part of our celebration of the liturgy as a Church.

Finding Meaning in Symbols

What kind of symbolic meaning can you find in the following natural signs? For example, light can mean knowledge.

Light

Darkness

Wind

Fire

Water

Tallis, or prayer shawl, worn by Jewish man or woman who has celebrated their Bar or Bat Mitzvah.

In the Christian tradition, Jesus also made known the mystery of God's covenant through words, actions, signs, and symbols. He performed healings and miracles, making known the power and presence of God. His death and resurrection is the Passover event, for the Christian, saving all people through the blood of the Lamb.

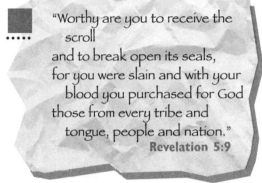

"Worthy are you to receive the scroll
and to break open its seals,
for you were slain and with your
    blood you purchased for God
those from every tribe and
    tongue, people and nation."
Revelation 5:9

Signs of the Covenant

One of the ways God established his covenant with the people of Israel was through signs and symbolic actions with religious meaning. These included consecration of priests, prophets, and kings with the anointing of oil and laying on of hands; sacrifices; and, above all, the Passover.

The writings of the Old Testament tell the story of God's covenant with the Chosen People. They contain many examples of God's blessings. Those stories of God's grace were, we believe, providential preparations for the New Covenant to be revealed and fulfilled in Christ. That is why the Church continues to incorporate the Old Testament prominently in our Liturgy of the Word, usually in the first reading and the responsorial psalm. The unity of the two covenants is found in the person of Jesus, God's greatest blessing of all.

Remembering the Covenant

The liturgy celebrates the Paschal mystery of Christ—his life, death, resurrection, and ascension. The words, gestures, and symbolic actions we use in the celebration of each part of the liturgy celebrate how individuals and the larger faith community are sharing in Christ's Paschal mystery.

Our liturgical signs and symbols help us remember God's presence and covenant with us. *Anamnesis* and *epiclesis* are two Greek words that help us deepen our understanding of what it means for the Church to gather as God's people and to remember his saving works among us. *Anamnesis* means "to remember" and *epiclesis* means "to summon," or "to invoke." Both words play key roles in our understanding of the Holy Spirit's role in the liturgy.

READING THE BIBLE

Choose two of these Scripture passages that recall blessings from God upon important people in the Old Testament. Read and reflect on the passages you select. Then summarize the story and explain the importance and promise of the blessings.

- ❏ Genesis 2:7–25 (Adam and Eve)
- ❏ Genesis 9:1–17 (Noah)
- ❏ Genesis 12:1–3 (Abraham)
- ❏ Genesis 17:1–14 (Circumcision)
- ❏ Genesis 22:1–18 (Abraham and Isaac)
- ❏ Exodus 12:1–30 (Passover)
- ❏ 1 Samuel 16:4–13 (David)
- ❏ 1 Kings 8:54–61; 9:1–9 (Temple)
- ❏ Jeremiah 31:31–34 (New Covenant)

First Story:

Second Story:

.... **Discuss:**

Name an important blessing you have received from God. How does it reveal God's covenant, or promise, to you?

Anamnesis. The prayer of anamnesis involves recalling God's saving actions as heard in the Word and prayers of the liturgy. It also makes the remembered events present in our midst once again. This means that in the Eucharist we not only recall Christ's death and resurrection, but also make his death and resurrection, his Paschal mystery, real in the present moment.

Epiclesis. In the epiclesis prayer we summon and invoke the Spirit. In the Eucharist the priest calls upon the Father to send the Holy Spirit so that the bread and wine may become the Body and Blood of Christ. It is the same Spirit called upon in the epiclesis that changes the people gathered into the Body of Christ. The Spirit unites us with Christ.

Our tradition has always understood that the Spirit *transforms* whatever and whomever he is invoked upon. Just as bread and wine become the Body and Blood of Christ, so we who gather in the liturgy are constituted as the Body of Christ by the power of the Holy Spirit.

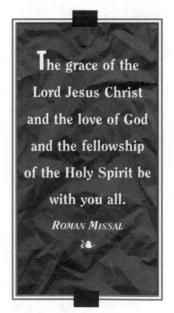

The grace of the Lord Jesus Christ and the love of God and the fellowship of the Holy Spirit be with you all.

ROMAN MISSAL

The Sacraments

The **sacraments** are "efficacious signs of grace, instituted by Christ and entrusted to the Church, by which divine life is dispensed to us. The visible rites by which the sacraments are celebrated signify and make present the graces proper to each sacrament" (CCC, 1131). The sacraments both instruct the faithful by words and actions and also "nourish, strengthen, and express faith" for everyone taking part in the celebration. For these reasons they are called sacraments of Christ, sacraments of the Church, sacraments of faith, sacraments of salvation, and sacraments of eternal life.

Sacraments of Christ
Sacraments of the Church

We believe that the words and actions of Jesus laid the foundation for the seven sacraments we celebrate today. By this we mean that these seven liturgical rituals are rooted in the ministry of Jesus and draw their saving power from the Paschal mystery of his death and resurrection. Thus we can say the seven sacraments, Baptism, Confirmation, the Eucharist, Penance (Reconciliation), Anointing of the Sick, Holy Orders, and Matrimony, were all "instituted" by Jesus.

The apostles continued this tradition and laid the foundation for the ordained ministry of the bishop, priest, or deacon who celebrates the sacraments today, in the place of Jesus himself. In 1547 the Council of Trent reaffirmed this tradition of seven sacraments by referring in its teaching to

What the Documents Say

The Second Vatican Council reminded us that the many liturgical traditions, or rites, in the Church are signs of the universality, or catholicity, of the Church. Each of these rites in its particular way is rooted in and faithful to the Apostolic Tradition. Each is a sign of, and makes present among us, the mystery of Christ.

Discuss:
The Roman, or Latin, Rite is the most widely celebrated rite of the Catholic Church. Research the other liturgical traditions, or rites, celebrated in the Catholic Church. Share a brief history of each. Point out similarities and differences in each rite.

the "teaching of the Holy Scriptures, to the apostolic traditions, and to the consensus . . . of the Fathers."

The three sacraments of Baptism, Confirmation, and Holy Orders leave a sacramental "character" or "seal" that remains with those who receive these sacraments for the rest of their life. These three sacraments are never to be repeated, and provide the person with an openness to grace, a promise and guarantee of divine protection, and a call to worship and to be of service to the Church and God's people.

Sacraments of Faith
Sacraments of Salvation

Two ancient Latin sayings summarize what we mean by the description "sacraments of faith." The first—*lex orandi, lex credendi*—means "The Church believes as she prays." The second, *ex opere operato,* means "by the very fact of the action being performed." Both these sayings tell us something very important about the sacraments.

Lex Orandi, Lex Credendi. This saying emphasizes that when we pray together in the liturgy, the faith of the Church is being put into action. When we celebrate the liturgy, we *do* what we *believe.* Sacraments are ways that the Church lives out its faith in God, who gives us birth in the Spirit, nourishes us with his own life, and heals us with divine power.

Ex Opere Operato. The second saying emphasizes that the effectiveness of a sacrament does not depend on the

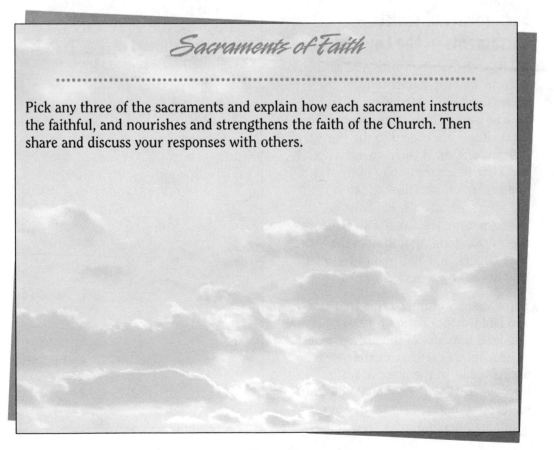

Sacraments of Faith

Pick any three of the sacraments and explain how each sacrament instructs the faithful, and nourishes and strengthens the faith of the Church. Then share and discuss your responses with others.

holiness of the minister who celebrates it. Rather, the sacraments are efficacious because *Christ* is their author and because in them Christ himself is at work (CCC, 1127). The sacrament is "effective" because it is the Body of Christ, Head and members, that performs the sacramental action, not just an individual person.

Catechesis. A third word, this time a Greek one, balances this emphasis on the faith of the whole Church. That word is **catechesis,** which means "to echo." Catechesis refers to the process of instruction and preparation for the sacraments in which a person is made ready to echo God's Word in their own life. We are catechized before we celebrate a sacrament so that we approach the liturgy with a faith that is alive and real. We speak of sacraments of faith because one who celebrates a sacrament should believe and live out the truth that Jesus comes to us in those special moments of grace.

Sacraments of Eternal Life

At the Last Supper Jesus told his disciples, "I have eagerly desired to eat this Passover with you before I suffer, for, I tell you, I shall not eat it [again] until there is fulfillment in the kingdom of God" (Luke 22:15). Christians since the time of the apostles have lived in that hope, crying out, "Maranatha! Come, Lord Jesus." In the celebration of the sacraments, we believe the Church already receives the guarantee of her inheritance and even now shares in everlasting life.

(CCC, 1066–1112)

The Role of the Trinity in the Liturgy and the Sacraments

All blessings come from God. Blessings are divine and life-giving actions that are both word and gift from God. In our relationship with God, *blessing* means adoration and surrender to God in thanksgiving. Paul often expressed this fundamental Christian attitude:

> Blessed be the God and Father of our Lord Jesus Christ, who has blessed us in Christ with every spiritual blessing in the heavens.
>
> **Ephesians 1:3**

God the Father of All Creation

It is in the Church's liturgy that God's blessings are fully revealed and communicated. God the Father is recognized as the source and end of all blessings. He has given us his Word made flesh, who died and rose for us and fills us with blessings. It is through the Word of God that we receive the blessings and gifts of the Holy Spirit.

Christian liturgy is a response of faith and love for the spiritual blessings that the Father unconditionally bestows upon us. We give thanks for what we have received.

The Son of God, Jesus Christ

Each liturgy participates in the prayer of Christ addressed to the Father in the Holy Spirit. Jesus is really and sacramentally present in the liturgy. He is present in the priest, in the proclamation of the Word, in the gathered assembly that makes up the Body of Christ, and in the Eucharist.

Each liturgy relives the Paschal mystery of Jesus, making Christ present and alive to each age of believers.

The Church is called to share in the work of Jesus. It shares in the priestly ministry of Jesus through worship, in the prophetic work of Jesus through the proclamation of the Word of God, and in the kingly ministry of Jesus through our service to love God, self, and neighbor through acts of charity.

The Holy Spirit

The presence and activity of the Holy Spirit is vital in every liturgical and sacramental celebration. The Holy Spirit:

❏ prepares the Church to encounter Jesus,

❏ recalls and makes Christ present to the faith of the assembly in the here and now,

❏ unites the Church to the life and mission of Christ.

The Holy Spirit prepares the Church to encounter Jesus through the fulfillment of the Old Covenant still present in the liturgy. We continue to listen to readings from the Old Testament. We sing psalms, recalling the saving events of God among the people of the Old Covenant, which is fulfilled in the mystery of Christ. These events include the promise and Covenant, the Exodus and Passover, the kingdom and Temple, and exile and return.

It is the Holy Spirit that unveils the mystery of Christ prepared for in the Old Testament and the life of the Israelites, the Chosen People. For example, the story of Noah's ark and the flood prefigures our salvation and rebirth in baptism. The story of the feeding of the Hebrews with manna in the desert prefigures the Eucharist, "the true bread from heaven."

Many activities in life involve some type of preparation, whether it is a test, a vacation or trip, or an athletic event. The Holy Spirit prepares both the faithful gathered and the leader of prayer to be well disposed for their participation in the liturgy.

> The grace of the Holy Spirit seeks to awaken faith, conversion of heart, and adherence to the Father's will. These dispositions are the precondition both for the reception of other graces conferred in the celebration itself and the fruits of new life which the celebration is intended to produce afterward.
>
> CCC, 1098

The Holy Spirit helps us hear, understand, and respond in faith to the proclamation of the Word of God. Hearing the Word of God does not stop with an understanding of the Word. Our response of faith includes concrete decisions and actions that enable us to live our life in Christ at home, at school, in our communities.

Sacramentals

Through the liturgy Christ's mystery of our salvation is made present by the power of the Holy Spirit. To help us prepare to receive the fruits of the sacraments and sanctify different circumstances of life, the Church has instituted sacred signs, which we call sacramentals.

Blessings are the most important of the sacramentals. "They include both praise of God for his works and gifts, and the Church's intercession for men that they may be able to use God's gifts according to the spirit of the Gospel" (CCC, 1678).

■
.... Discuss:
Brainstorm a list of the sacramentals (objects and blessings that you know about. Select one and describe its meaning for you, your family, or your parish community.

Prayer

❖ ❖ ❖

Each eucharistic prayer contains the epiclesis prayer, which calls upon the Holy Spirit to sanctify the bread and wine that they may become the Body and Blood of Jesus. This epiclesis prayer is taken from Eucharistic Prayer III. Read and prayerfully reflect on this prayer, being attentive to the unique roles of the Father, the Son, and the Holy Spirit:

> **Father, you are holy indeed,**
> **and all creation rightly gives you praise.**
> **All life, all holiness comes from you**
> **through your Son, Jesus Christ our Lord,**
> **by the working of the Holy Spirit.**
> **From age to age you gather a people to yourself,**
> **so that from east to west**
> **a perfect offering may be made**
> **to the glory of your name.**
>
> **And so, Father, we bring you these gifts.**
> **We ask you to make them holy by the power of your Spirit**
> **that they may become the body + and blood**
> **of your Son, our Lord Jesus Christ,**
> **at whose command we celebrate this eucharist.**
>
> *ROMAN MISSAL*

IMPORTANT TERMS TO KNOW

· ·

anamnesis—a Greek word meaning "recalling, remembering"; making present the saving events of Jesus' death and resurrection in the here and now

catechesis—a Greek word meaning "to echo"; it is used by the Church to describe the instruction of those preparing for the sacraments, resulting in conversion and a changed way of life.

epiclesis—a Greek word meaning "invoking, calling down"; the calling down of the Holy Spirit upon the bread and wine to change them into the Body and Blood of Jesus Christ, at whose command we celebrate the Eucharist

ex opere operato—a Latin saying that means "by the very fact of the action being performed"; the holiness of those celebrating or receiving the sacrament does not determine the power of the sacrament itself. The sacraments are efficacious because *Christ* is their author and because in them Christ himself is at work (CCC, 1127).

lex orandi, lex credendi—a Latin saying that means "The Church believes as she prays"; this adage stresses that our liturgy celebrates the faith of the Church.

sacraments—efficacious signs of grace, instituted by Christ and entrusted to the Church, by which divine life is dispensed to us

CHAPTER SUMMARY

The sacraments celebrate and allow us to take part in the Paschal mystery of Christ. In this chapter we learned:

1. A symbol is a sign with many meanings.

2. Human communication through language, gestures, and actions is also used to communicate with God.

3. The seven sacraments that were instituted by Jesus are Baptism, Confirmation, the Eucharist, Penance, Anointing of the Sick, Holy Orders, and Matrimony.

4. The Old Covenant was fulfilled through the life, death, and resurrection of Jesus Christ, whose words, signs, and actions point to and reveal the mystery of God.

5. The Father, the Son, and the Holy Spirit are present and active in each liturgical and sacramental celebration. The Father is the source of all blessings and calls for a response of thanks and praise and acts of charity.

6. In Jesus, the Son, the Paschal mystery is made present in the celebration of the sacraments, and we share in his mission as priests, prophets, and kings.

7. The Holy Spirit has the threefold task of preparing the Church to encounter Jesus, of recalling and making Christ present to the faithful assembled here and now, and of uniting the Church to the mission of Christ.

EXPLORING OUR CATHOLIC FAITH

1. Listening to God's Word
Read and reflect on Jeremiah 31:31–34. What is the promise that God makes with his people? What will you do to keep that promise?

2. Understanding the Teachings of the Catholic Church
The Second Vatican Council taught many things about the sacraments and the liturgy. Among those teachings is the following:

[B]y the saving Word of God faith is . . . nourished in the heart of believers. By this faith then the congregation of the faithful begins and grows.
Decree on the Ministry and Life of Priests, 4

Discuss ways the proclamation of the Word of God at the celebration of the Eucharist nourishes the faith of the worshiping community and the faith of individual members of the assembly.

3. Reflecting on Our Catholic Faith
Saint Ambrose, who was bishop of Milan, Italy, from 374 to 397, often wrote on the sacraments. He shares this insight with us: "We must always meditate on God's wisdom, keeping it in our hearts and on our lips. Your lips must speak justice, the law of God must be in your heart." Reflect on how Ambrose's insight helps you respond in faith to your participation in the liturgy. Write your reflections in your journal.

4. Living Our Catholic Faith
At the end of the celebration of Mass we are dismissed with the words: "Go in peace to love and serve the Lord" *(Roman Missal).* What are some ways you can do this? By doing these things, in what ways are you a sign of God's presence with and love for all people?

CHAPTER 4

Baptism

"Go, therefore, and make disciples of all nations, baptizing them in the name of the Father, and of the Son, and of the holy Spirit, teaching them to observe all that I have commanded you."

MATTHEW 28:19–20

There are many similarities between the stages and events of our natural life and those of our spiritual life. What are some of those similarities? List your ideas here.

Maria had worked hard for this moment. Standing before the judge, she proudly pledged her allegiance to the United States. When Maria came to the United States, her heart was filled with dreams and hopes. She had worked hard, spending nights learning English and studying the duties and rights of American citizenship. Her supervisor at the day care center where she worked and her neighbors witnessed to her character and her work. She had taken the test and passed it with flying colors. Now, on September 17, Citizenship Day, she was ready to take the United States oath of allegiance. She was ready to become a naturalized citizen.

What does it mean to become a citizen or a responsible member of any group or organization?

Why do groups have a period of **initiation** or discernment as part of bringing new members into the group?

KEY TERMS

Baptism

catechumenate

initiation

mystagogy

neophytes

Rite of Christian Initiation of Adults (RCIA)

New citizens taking naturalization oath at citizenship ceremony.

nitiation is a word that refers to the process of being "admitted" to a group or an organization. It usually involves a process of preparation, instruction, or testing. The initiation process helps both the group and the individuals seeking membership in the group. The Church welcomes new members through a process of initiation, which culminates in the celebration of the sacraments of Christian initiation: Baptism, Confirmation, and the Eucharist. "Baptism which is the beginning of new life; Confirmation which is its strengthening; and the Eucharist which nourishes the disciple with Christ's Body and Blood for his transformation in Christ" (CCC, 1275). In this chapter we will explore the meaning and celebration of Baptism, the first of the Sacraments of Christian Initiation.

(*Catechism of the Catholic Church,* 1229–1233)

Christian Initiation

From the time of the apostles, becoming a Christian has involved a journey through several stages that could be covered rapidly or slowly. This process contains certain essential elements: proclamation of the Word of God, acceptance of the Gospel, conversion, profession of faith, Baptism itself, the outpouring of the Holy Spirit, and the admission to eucharistic communion.

Today, the Church invites adults and school-age children who wish to become members of the Catholic Church to take part in the **Rite of Christian Initiation of Adults (RCIA),** the Church's initiation process. This

process is a spiritual journey that the Church makes with the catechumens, those seeking membership in the Catholic Church.

Participation in the Rite of Christian Initiation of Adults may last for several years. It consists of four "periods" and three "steps," or rites that mark significant moments on the journey.

Period of Evangelization and Precatechumenate

The first period is a time of evangelization, a time in which the Church constantly proclaims "the living God and Jesus Christ whom he has sent for the salvation of all" (RCIA, 36). It is a time when God invites both those seeking membership in the Church and the faithful who welcome them to open their hearts to the Holy Spirit and to commit themselves to Christ.

Inquirers who are being evangelized in the precatechumenate may take a shorter or longer time to come to initial conversion. And so the Church must constantly offer the ministry to all who approach seeking membership.

First Step: Rite of Acceptance into the Order of Catechumens. The first step is the celebration of the Rite of Acceptance into the Order of Catechumens. This takes place after both those seeking membership in the Church and those responsible for the precatechumenate process agree upon their readiness.

Once this rite has been celebrated, the inquirers are called catechumens. They enter into a new and real relationship with the Church by participating in the **catechumenate.**

Period of the Catechumenate

The Period of the Catechumenate may last from several months to several years. Those seeking initiation into the Church join with the faithful—their sponsors, godparents, catechists, deacons, priests, and other members of the parish—to study, live, and celebrate the Christian life.

This is done in four ways. First, the teachings and precepts of the Church are studied. Second, with the faithful as their guides, they set out on a spiritual journey. They learn "to turn more readily to God in prayer, to bear witness to the faith, . . . to keep their hopes set on Christ, to follow supernatural inspiration in their deeds, and to practice love of neighbor, even at the cost of self-renunciation" (RCIA, 75.2).

Third, they participate in the Liturgy of the Word at Mass and in the celebration of other rites, which strengthen their conversion with God's blessings. During this time they learn to pray as Catholics pray by joining with the members of the faithful at prayer.

Fourth, they work "actively with others to spread the Gospel and build up the Church by the witness of their lives and by professing their faith" (RCIA, 75.4).

Second Step: Rite of Election or Enrollment of Names. The second step, the celebration of the Rite of Election or Enrollment of Names, closes the Period of the Catechumenate. This rite is usually celebrated at the beginning of Lent and "marks the beginning of the period of final, more intense preparation for the sacraments of initiation, during which the elect will be encouraged to follow Christ with greater generosity" (RCIA, 118).

Signed as Christ's Disciples

During the Rite of Acceptance into the Order of Catechumens, the celebrant signs the forehead of those being admitted as catechumens. As he signs each one, he says:

> (Name), receive the cross on your forehead.
> It is Christ himself who now strengthens you
> with this sign of his love.
> Learn to know him and follow him.
> RCIA, 55

During our life we often sign ourselves and are signed with the cross. In what ways are you learning to know Christ and to follow Christ?

.... Discuss:
Compare your efforts to know and follow Christ with your efforts at learning about mathematics and science. How do you interpret your response?

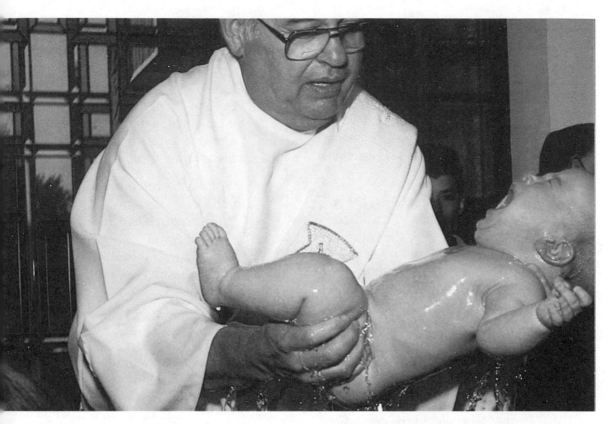

At this step the Church "elects," or chooses, those to be baptized at Easter and helps them prepare and advance toward full initiation into the Church.

Period of Purification and Enlightenment

The Period of Purification and Enlightenment usually coincides with Lent. As we have seen in chapter 1, during this season those who have been baptized prepare to renew their baptism and those preparing for the sacrament of Baptism prepare more intensely for its reception. It is a time of repentance and renewal, a time to enter into and celebrate the Paschal mystery of Christ's death-resurrection-ascension.

Third Step: Celebration of the Sacraments of Initiation. The third step is the celebration of the Sacraments of Initiation at the Easter Vigil. The elect enter into full membership in the Church. Those who have already been baptized in another Christian faith are not baptized a second time.

Mystagogy, or Period of Postbaptismal Catechesis

The newly initiated members of the Church are called **neophytes,** a word that comes from a Greek word meaning "new growth." During this period, which coincides with the fifty days of the Easter season, the entire church community welcomes the neophytes. Together, they deepen their understanding of their participation in the Paschal mystery of Christ. "Out of this experience . . . they derive a new perception of the faith, of the Church, and of the world" (RCIA, 245).

A Word about Candidates

In many places there are individuals who were previously baptized in another Christian tradition or may have been baptized into the Catholic Church but who never received any instruction in the faith. They now wish to be prepared to complete their initiation through the sacraments of Confirmation and the Eucharist. Such individuals are called candidates.

Candidates should participate in the initiation process of the catechumenate alongside those preparing for Baptism. The rituals are adapted to suit the status of the candidates. But the catechetical instruction is the same, seeking conversion of heart and mind to Christ and a commitment to live out one's faith as a member of the Church.

(CCC, 1213–1261)

Baptism

B **aptism** celebrates our birth into new life in Christ and forms us into God's people.

The Sacrament of Baptism

Baptism is the most important of all the sacraments because it is "the door to life and to the kingdom of God, . . . the first sacrament of the New Law, which Christ offered to all that they might have eternal life" (*Christian Initiation*, General Introduction, 3).

The word *baptism* comes from a Greek word meaning "to plunge," or "to immerse." In Baptism we are immersed into water. This symbolizes our burial into the death of Christ and our rising up to new life in Christ. From the very

READING THE BIBLE

Read and reflect on this passage from the New Testament Letter to the Philippians:

> Have among yourselves the same attitude that is also yours in Christ Jesus,
>
> Who, though he was in the form of God,
>   did not regard equality with God
>   something to be grasped.
>   Rather, he emptied himself,
>   taking the form of a slave,
>   coming in human likeness;
>   and found human in appearance,
>   he humbled himself,
>   becoming obedient to death,
>   even death on a cross.
>
> Philippians 2:5–8

.... Discuss:

In what ways can Christians become one in mind with Christ? List several ideas and explain how each can achieve that goal.

beginning of the Church, this has been the Church's belief about Baptism. Saint Paul wrote:

> Or are you unaware that we who were baptized into Christ Jesus were baptized into his death? We were indeed buried with him through baptism into death, so that, just as Christ was raised from the dead by the glory of the Father, we too might live in newness of life. **Romans 6:3–4**

The Son of God became man, suffered, died, and was raised from the dead for all people. We are all called to one and the same destiny—to share in the life and love of God.

The Baptism of Jesus. At Jesus' baptism by John the Baptist, the Gospel according to Matthew tells of the Spirit of God coming upon Jesus (Matthew 3:13–17). This gospel story, which is told in all four gospels, not only begins Jesus' public ministry, or work among the people; but the story of the sacrament of Baptism as well.

The Commissioning of the Disciples. Before his ascension and return to the Father, Jesus gathered the apostles and sent them forth to make disciples of all peoples.

> "Go, therefore, and make disciples of all nations, baptizing them in the name of the Father, and of the Son, and of the holy Spirit, teaching them to observe all that I have commanded you. And behold, I am with you always, until the end of the age." **Matthew 28:19–20**

The Church, from the very beginning, has focused on this commission as the heart of her work among people. The Church has always preached that

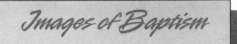

Images of Baptism

Saint Gregory of Nazianus, who was bishop of Constantinople from 375 to 381, described Baptism this way:

> Baptism is God's most beautiful and magnificent gift. . . . We call it gift, grace, anointing, enlightenment, garment of immortality, bath of rebirth, seal, and most precious gift. It is called *gift* because it is conferred on those who bring nothing of their own; *grace* since it is given even to the guilty; *Baptism* because sin is buried in the water; *anointing* for it is priestly and royal as are those who are anointed; *enlightenment* because it radiates light; *clothing* since it veils our shame; *bath* because it washes; and *seal* as it is our guard and the sign of God's lordship.

Discuss:

List the images Gregory gives for Baptism.

What does each say to you about Baptism?

Jesus is at the center of God's plan of loving salvation for all people. In Christ, all have been saved and reconciled with God.

Everyone, however, may not have the opportunity to be baptized. This does not close the door to their entering the kingdom of God. "[T]he Holy Spirit offers to all the possibility of being made partners, in a way known to God, of the Paschal mystery" (*Constitution on the Church in the Modern World,* 22).

Here are three examples of people who, although not baptized, still can experience salvation:

❑ Martyrs, or those who are put to death for their faith, receive what is called "Baptism of blood." The Church considers them baptized by their death for and with Christ.

❑ Catechumens—those being instructed in the faith, and even those who merely desire Baptism but who die before they are baptized —are offered salvation by their desire to receive it, their repentance for their sins, and acts of charity. This is called the "Baptism of desire."

❑ Children or infants who die before they are baptized are entrusted to the mercy of God. Jesus' love and care for children reflect the mercy and love of God. This is the basis of our hope that such little ones can enjoy the grace of heaven despite their lack of Baptism. The *Catechism* says, "God has bound salvation to the sacrament of Baptism, but he himself is not bound by his sacraments" (CCC, 1257).

The Rite of Baptism

After his resurrection Jesus commissioned his apostles to make disciples of all nations by baptizing them "in the name of the Father, and of the Son, and of the holy Spirit" (Matthew 28:19).

The Baptism of Adults. The Acts of the Apostles, the New Testament letters, and other early Christians writings clearly teach that the Church has carried out this command since the time of the apostles. In the Acts of the Apostles we read about the baptism of:

❑ over three thousand on the first Christian Pentecost (Acts 2:41),

❑ the baptism of Lydia and her household (Acts 16:15),

❑ the jailer and his household (Acts 16:33), and

❑ Crispus, the synagogue official and his entire household (Acts 18:8).

From the beginning any adult who accepted faith in Jesus and was willing to undergo the Church's initiation process was eligible for Baptism. During the early centuries, the catechumenate was the normal process for Christian initiation. But then for nearly 1,500 years, right up until when the Second Vatican Council (1962–1965) restored it, catechetical preparation disappeared. It is only in recent years that the Church has restored the catechumenate as the ordinary way to initiate adults and children of school age.

The Baptism of Infants. The Baptism of infants is rooted in the Baptism of entire families that chose to be Christian and be baptized in the early Church. Parents commit to raise and teach the child faith in Jesus Christ. The Church emphasizes that the infant

The writers of Sacred Scripture often use water as a symbol that helps us understand a deeper truth the writer is trying to hand on to us. Read and reflect on these Scripture passages. In each of them water is used as a symbol. In the space provided, describe how each passage helps you understand the meaning of the mystery of Baptism.

Genesis 1:2

John 4:4–15

Genesis 6:5–13, 18–22

.... Discuss:
Why does the use of water in Baptism help us understand the mystery that is taking place before us?

Exodus 14:10

will need a "postbaptismal catechumenate," that is, further instruction in order to grow in grace.

In the Eastern tradition, which still follows the Church's most ancient custom in this matter, infants receive all three of the Sacraments of Initiation, but in the Roman Church the sacraments of Confirmation and the Eucharist are delayed until later. Oftentimes, the original sequence is also changed to allow the reception of the Eucharist before Confirmation. But this is still seen as an exception to the norm.

The Mystagogy of the Rite of Baptism

The Greek word **mystagogy** is another word that refers to "instruction" or "ongoing instruction" after celebrating the sacraments. By looking at the parts of the baptismal rite, we can learn much more about the deeper meaning of the mystery of Baptism.

The Sign of the Cross. The signing with the cross marks the body of the one to be baptized as one who will soon belong to Christ, who died on the cross and achieved victory over sin and death. This gesture is done by the celebrant, parents, and godparents for infants. With adults it occurs during the Rite of Acceptance into the Order of Catechumens.

The Proclamation of the Word. Proclaiming the Word enlightens the candidates and the assembly with the revealed truth and elicits the response of faith.

Blessing and Invocation of God over the Water. A prayer of epiclesis consecrates the baptismal water. The Church asks God that through his Son the power of the Holy Spirit may be sent upon the water. We ask that those who will be baptized in it may be "born of water and Spirit" (John 3:5).

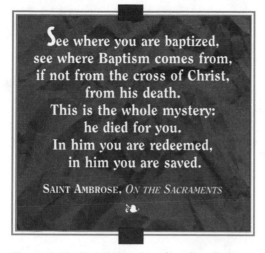

Exorcism. Baptism signifies freedom from sin and the instigator of sin, the devil. Because of this, one or more exorcisms or prayers protecting the person from evil are said.

Anointing with the Oil of Catechumens. This gesture signifies both strength and protection, which the one to be baptized draws from the Church.

Renunciation of Sin and Profession of Faith. These are the most solemn vows an individual makes. Parents and godparents are asked to make them on behalf of an infant, while adults do so in their own name.

Baptism. The essential rite of the sacrament involves being immersed in the water three times or having water poured over the candidate's head three times while the minister says the words, "(Name), I baptize you in the name of the Father, and of the Son, and of the Holy Spirit."

Anointing with Chrism. The person is then anointed with sacred chrism, the perfumed oil consecrated by the bishop. The anointing signifies the gift of the Holy Spirit to the newly baptized, who has become a Christian, that is, one "anointed" by the Holy Spirit, becoming one with Christ who is priest, prophet, and king.

Clothing with White Garment. A white garment is worn, or put on by the person, symbolizing that the person baptized has "put on Christ," and has risen with Christ.

Lighted Candle. A candle, lighted from the Paschal candle, signifies that Christ has enlightened the neophytes. The "light of the world" is now within them.

(CCC, 1262–1274)

The Grace of Baptism

Baptism is a sacrament that is not to be repeated.

The Seal of Baptism

The baptized receive an indelible, spiritual mark, or character. This mark seals the baptized as belonging to Christ and can never be erased by sin. It enables and commits the baptized to participate in the liturgy of the Church and to exercise their baptismal priesthood by the witness of holy lives and acts of charity.

This seal is also the seal of the Holy Spirit, the seal of the Lord "for the day of redemption." It is the seal of eternal life, which we are promised through our baptism. It is the sign of faith, which we are called to keep throughout our life until we reach our destination and receive the hope of the Resurrection.

The Effects of Baptism

A number of things happen when we celebrate the sacrament of Baptism. Through Baptism we are purified from

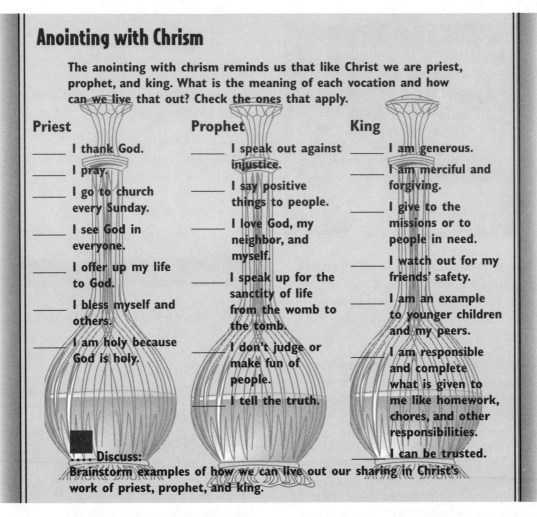

Anointing with Chrism

The anointing with chrism reminds us that like Christ we are priest, prophet, and king. What is the meaning of each vocation and how can we live that out? Check the ones that apply.

Priest

_____ I thank God.

_____ I pray.

_____ I go to church every Sunday.

_____ I see God in everyone.

_____ I offer up my life to God.

_____ I bless myself and others.

_____ I am holy because God is holy.

Prophet

_____ I speak out against injustice.

_____ I say positive things to people.

_____ I love God, my neighbor, and myself.

_____ I speak up for the sanctity of life from the womb to the tomb.

_____ I don't judge or make fun of people.

_____ I tell the truth.

King

_____ I am generous.

_____ I am merciful and forgiving.

_____ I give to the missions or to people in need.

_____ I watch out for my friends' safety.

_____ I am an example to younger children and my peers.

_____ I am responsible and complete what is given to me like homework, chores, and other responsibilities.

_____ I can be trusted.

.... Discuss: Brainstorm examples of how we can live out our sharing in Christ's work of priest, prophet, and king.

sins, receive new life in the Holy Spirit, are reborn as adopted children of God, and become members of the Body of Christ.

Forgiveness of Sin. Water is an element used to wash, cleanse, and bathe. Through Baptism all sins are washed away: original sin, personal sin, and all punishment for sin. Baptism does not prevent us from experiencing suffering, illness, death, and weakness of character. Concupiscence, or the inclination to sin, is something the baptized will wrestle with throughout their life.

New Creature. "Baptism not only purifies from all sins, but also makes the neophyte 'a new creature,' an adopted son of God, who has become a 'partaker of the divine nature' (2 Corinthians 5:17; 2 Peter 1:4; Galatians 4:5–7), member of Christ and co-heir with him (1 Corinthians 6:15; 12:27; Romans 8:17), and a temple of the Holy Spirit (1 Corinthians 6:19)" (CCC, 1265).

Through Baptism we are reborn by water and the Spirit. Where the first children of God, Adam and Eve, lost the promise through sin, the children of the new Adam, Christ, are reborn as heirs of the promise. Baptism makes us God's children in a special way by giving us a share in his own life.

Just as each sacrament gives the person "sacramental grace," the Most Holy Trinity gives the baptized "sanctifying grace," or the grace of justification. This grace enables the person to believe in God, to hope in God, and to love God.

It gives the baptized the power to live and act under the prompting of the Holy Spirit through the gifts of the Holy Spirit. It allows them to grow in goodness through courage, justice, honesty, wise judgment, and peacemaking.

Members of the Body of Christ. Baptism makes us members of the Body of Christ, members of one another. It incorporates us into the Church. We become members "of the New Covenant, which transcends all the natural or human limits of nations, cultures, races, and sexes: 'For by one Spirit we were all baptized into one body' (1 Corinthians 12:13)" (CCC, 1267).

Through Baptism we become "living stones" to be "built into a spiritual house to be a holy priesthood" (1 Peter 2:5). The baptized are " 'a chosen race, a royal priesthood, a holy nation, a people of his own' " (1 Peter 2:9). Through Baptism we no longer belong to ourselves but to Christ who died and rose for us. (See 1 Corinthians 6:19, 2 Corinthians 5:15.)

As members of the Church we are to be of service to others and to obey the teachings and authority of the leaders of the Church. We also enjoy rights within the Church:

❏ to receive the sacraments,

❏ to be nourished by the Word of God, and

❏ to be sustained by the other spiritual helps of the Church.

Unity of all Christians

Baptism unites all Christians as members of the one Body of Christ. This includes those living in full communion with the Catholic Church and those not yet in full communion with her.

The unity of the Holy Trinity—one God in three Persons—is the basis of the Church's unity. The Church is one because of her founder, Jesus Christ, and because of her soul, the one who gives her life, the Holy Spirit. All Christians—Catholic and non-Catholic—must continually pray for perfect unity in the Church. There is "one Lord, one faith, one baptism"; Paul writes, "one God and Father of all, who is over all and through all and in all" (Ephesians 4:6). Into this great mystery of God's love, we are baptized.

Q & A

Who can baptize?
CCC, 1256

The ordinary ministers of Baptism are the bishop, priest, and deacon. In case of emergency, any person, even one not baptized, can baptize another by sincerely saying the Trinitarian baptismal formula. The Church allows this due to the importance of Baptism for salvation.

.... Discuss:
How would you baptize someone if it were necessary for you to do so?

Prayer

❖ ❖ ❖

Blessing of Water

This prayer, which is part of the prayer that is prayed over the water by the celebrant at the Easter Vigil, helps us understand and live our baptism.

> Father, you give us grace
> through sacramental signs,
> which tell us of the wonders of
> your unseen power.
> In baptism we use your gift of
> water, which you have made a
> rich symbol of the grace you
> give us in this sacrament.
> At the very dawn of creation
> your Spirit breathed on the
> waters, making them the
> wellspring of all holiness. . . .
> Your Son willed that water and
> blood should flow from his
> side as he hung upon the
> cross. . . .
> Father, look now with love upon
> your Church and unseal for it
> the fountain of baptism.
> By the power of the Spirit
> give to the water of this font
> the grace of your Son. . . .
> We ask you, Father, with your
> Son to send the Holy Spirit
> upon the waters of this font.
> May all who are buried with
> Christ in the death of baptism
> rise to newness of life.
>
> *ROMAN MISSAL*

IMPORTANT TERMS TO KNOW

Baptism—from the Greek word meaning to "plunge" or "immerse"; the Sacrament of Initiation in which we become members of the Church and adopted children of God, original sin and all personal sins are forgiven, and we receive the gift of the Holy Spirit

catechumenate—the process of instruction and conversion that leads to Baptism

initiation—the process of being admitted into an organization, group, or church

mystagogy—from the Greek word for "instruction" or "ongoing instruction" after celebrating the sacrament

neophytes—from the word for "new growth"; the newly baptized

Rite of Christian Initiation of Adults (RCIA)—the process by which the Church initiates adults and school-age children into the Church

CHAPTER SUMMARY

Baptism is one of the three Sacraments of Initiation. It marks the start of the Christian's sacramental life and contains the promise of salvation. In this chapter we learned:

1. The initiation process by which the Church initiates adults and school-age children into the Church is call the Rite of Christian Initiation of Adults (RCIA). The Sacraments of Initiation are Baptism, Confirmation, and the Eucharist.

2. The tradition of baptizing infants is rooted in the early Church, where entire families were baptized and brought into the Church.

3. The Rite of Baptism includes signing a person with the cross, proclaiming the Word of God, saying prayers of exorcism, anointing with the oil of catechumens, pouring water and saying the words of the Trinitarian formula, anointing with chrism, receiving a white garment and lighted candle.

4. A person may be baptized only once. The baptized receive an indelible mark that seals them for the day of redemption.

5. The ordinary ministers of Baptism are the bishop, priest, and deacon. In case of emergency, any person, even one not baptized, can baptize by using water and the Trinitarian formula.

6. The effects of Baptism are purification from sins and new birth in the Holy Spirit. We share in the priestly, prophetic, and kingly ministry of Christ. The baptized become new creatures, members of the Body of Christ, and are called to serve others and obey the authority of the Church.

7. All Christians are united in Baptism.

EXPLORING OUR CATHOLIC FAITH

1. Listening to God's Word

The Church names several readings from Sacred Scripture to be used for the celebration of Baptism. Here are some of those readings: Ezekiel 36:24–28, Matthew 25: 35–40, John 3:1–6, John 15:1–11, Romans 8:28–32, and Galatians 3:26–28. Choose two of these readings. Prayerfully read them and share what they say about the meaning of the mystery of Baptism.

2. Understanding the Teachings of the Catholic Church

The Church teaches, "Through baptism we are formed in the likeness of Christ" (*Constitution on the Church*, 4). Using what has been presented in this chapter, explain what that teaching means.

3. Reflecting on Our Catholic Faith

Throughout the centuries Baptism has been called a bath. How does that image help you understand the mystery of Baptism? Write your reflections in your journal.

4. Living Our Catholic Faith

Baptism is birth into the new life in Christ. Baptism makes us members of the Body of Christ, members of one another. Brainstorm ways you are giving witness to that belief. What else can you do?

CHAPTER 5
Confirmation

"The spirit of the Lord will rush upon you,
and you . . . will be changed."
1 SAMUEL 10:6

What Do You Think?

Give the reasons why you agree or disagree with this statement: Those who have been baptized continue on the path of Christian initiation through the sacrament of Confirmation.

Recently, a doctor was speaking on a Christian radio station about how he was responsible for 75,000 abortions. While he was an abortionist he also became very active in the movement to make abortion legal in the United States.

But something began to happen to him. After the sonogram and fetal heartbeat monitoring came widely into use, he came face-to-face with the unborn child. He came to realize that abortion, in its many forms, is actually the cruel and brutal murder of unborn children. He had a complete change of heart and became a strong pro-life advocate for the unborn.

How can you explain the change that took place in this particular doctor? Was it the work of the Holy Spirit? Explain your opinion.

Relief of *Conversion of Paul.*
Michelangelo (1475–1564)

The doctor in the opening story underwent a life-changing experience.

We believe that the Holy Spirit, with the Father and the Son, changes the lives of people. In the New Testament, Saul was changed on his way to Damascus to arrest Christians. He was struck by a blinding light and heard the voice of Jesus saying, "Saul, Saul, why are you persecuting me?" (Acts of the Apostles 9:4)

The celebration of Confirmation is a celebration of our faith in the Holy Spirit. After Baptism, along with the Eucharist, it completes the baptismal graces and fully initiates the baptized into the Catholic Church. In this chapter we will explore the meaning of the sacrament of Confirmation.

(Catechism of the Catholic Church, 1286–1289)

The Holy Spirit in the Scriptures

The Church's belief in the active presence of the Spirit with us and among us is central to Christianity. This belief is clearly revealed in Sacred Scripture and in the teachings of the apostles.

Old Testament

The Book of Genesis, at the beginning of the Bible, speaks of the Spirit of God as "a mighty wind" that swept over the waters (Genesis 1:2). The Hebrew word translated "wind" in this passage can also be translated "spirit." Later in the Old Testament, we read about the Spirit of the Lord in the writings of the prophets who speak of the Spirit who would rest on the hoped-for **Messiah.**

The Holy Spirit in Our Lives

Give examples of what you can do to spread the faith by word and deed.

New Testament

In the Gospel of Luke, we read that Jesus was conceived by the Holy Spirit (Luke 1:35). At his baptism by John the Baptist, the Gospel according to Matthew tells of the Spirit of God coming upon Jesus (Matthew 3:13–17, John 1:33–34). In the synagogue in Nazareth Jesus, echoing the prophet Isaiah, announces to his listeners, "The Spirit of the Lord is upon me."

The whole life and mission of Jesus given to him by his Father would be lived out in union with the Holy Spirit. And before his ascension, he promised that the same Spirit would come and be with his disciples, as their Advocate and Teacher.

The Pentecost Story

There is no greater story about the Holy Spirit than the **Pentecost** story in Acts of the Apostles 2:1–13. During his preaching to the crowds gathered in Jerusalem for the celebration of Pentecost, Peter states how a person must change, or be converted, before receiving the Spirit. "Repent and be baptized," he says, "every one of you, in the name of Jesus Christ for the forgiveness of your sins; and you will receive the gift of the holy Spirit" (Acts of the Apostles 2:38).

(CCC, 1288–1289, 1293–1314)

The Celebration of Confirmation

Through the centuries the Rite of Confirmation, or the conferring of the gifts of the Holy Spirit, has been celebrated in many ways. In our time the sacrament of Confirmation:

is conferred through the anointing with **chrism** on the forehead, which is done by the laying on of the hand, and through the words: Be sealed with the gift of the Holy Spirit.

Apostolic Constitution on the Sacrament of Confirmation, 19

Sayings about the Holy Spirit

Look up and read these Scripture passages. Then in the space under each passage, describe what that passage says about the promise of God's Spirit on all God's people.

Ezekiel 36:25–27

Joel 3:1–2

Luke 12:12

John 7:37–39

John 16:7–15

Acts 1:8

.... **Discuss:**

Whether we cooperate with the Spirit or not, the Spirit is with us. Brainstorm ways that can help us be aware of the Spirit's presence in our lives.

The symbolic actions of the anointing with oil and the laying on of hands both show and make present what is happening in the celebration of the sacrament of Confirmation.

The Anointing with Chrism

The significance of anointing with oil is seen in the Eastern Churches. They refer to this sacrament both as **chrismation,** or anointing with chrism, and as **myron,** which means chrism. The Western, or Latin, Churches refer to it as Confirmation, the sacrament which ratifies Baptism and strengthens the grace of Baptism.

The anointing with chrism is connected to the name *Christian,* which means the "anointed ones." The title **Christ** is Greek for "Anointed One," as is *Messiah,* which is the Hebrew equivalent for "Anointed One." In his instruction to Cornelius, Peter describes Jesus as anointed by God. We read:

"You know the word [that] he sent to the Israelites as he proclaimed peace through Jesus Christ, who is Lord of all, what has happened all over Judea, beginning in Galilee after the baptism that John preached, how God anointed Jesus of Nazareth with the holy Spirit and power."
Acts of the Apostles 10:36–38

In Sacred Scripture oil, like water, is a symbol with many meanings. It is an image that points to abundance and joy—it cleanses before and after a bath; it limbers the body and muscles for athletes and wrestlers; it soothes and heals bruises and wounds; and it makes one radiant with beauty, health, and strength.

The parable of the Good Samaritan mentions "oil and wine" (Luke 10:34) that is poured into the wounds of the man beaten, robbed, and left for dead.

Psalm 23, the widely used Good Shepherd Psalm, joyfully proclaims:

> You anoint my head with oil;
> my cup overflows. **Psalm 23:5**

All of these deeper meanings are present when oil is used in sacramental celebrations.

❏ Anointing with the oil of catechumens at Baptism signifies cleansing and strengthening.

❏ Anointing of the sick with the oil of the sick signifies healing and comfort.

❏ Anointing with chrism at Baptism and Confirmation and Holy Orders signifies consecration and service to the mission of Jesus Christ.

The Tradition of Laying On of Hands

In Acts of the Apostles we read of Peter and John laying, or imposing, their hands on the Samaritans as they receive the Spirit.

> Then they laid hands on them and they received the holy Spirit.
>
> **Acts of the Apostles 8:17**

This experience is so impressive that Simon the Magician offers money to Peter and John to buy the power. "Give me this power too," he asks, "so that anyone upon whom I lay my hands may receive the holy Spirit" (Acts of the Apostles 8:19).

The Spiritual Seal

A mark, or seal, was a sign of personal authority or ownership of an object. Soldiers were marked with the sign of their leader's seal, and slaves were marked with the seal of their master. Seals were used to make documents official.

READING THE BIBLE

Read and reflect on Isaiah 61:1–2 and Luke 4:16–22. Give examples of how Jesus fulfilled the prophecy of Isaiah.

To bring glad tidings to the poor

To proclaim liberty to captives

and recovery of sight to the blind

To let the oppressed go free

To proclaim a year acceptable to the Lord

.... Discuss:

Compare the message in Isaiah and Luke with the life of a confirmed Christian.

The New Testament tells us Jesus himself was marked with the seal of God. In speaking of his work to the Pharisees, Jesus says:

> "Do not work for food that perishes but for the food that endures for eternal life, which the Son of Man will give you. For on him the Father, God, has set his seal."
>
> **John 6:27**

The New Testament also speaks of Christians as being marked with the seal of the Holy Spirit—belonging completely to God and Christ.

> But the one who gives us security with you in Christ and who anointed us is God; he has also put his seal upon us and given the Spirit in our hearts.
>
> **2 Corinthians 1:21–22**

Confirmation, like Baptism, is conferred only once. It leaves an indelible mark, or seal or character, of Jesus Christ upon the person. It clothes the person with the Holy Spirit to exercise the common priesthood of the faithful, received at Baptism, and to publicly and officially profess faith in Christ. We believe that this seal is indelible—we can never lose it. We belong to Christ forever. We commit ourselves to him and his service forever.

Who Should Receive Confirmation?

Without the sacrament of Confirmation the baptized person is not fully initiated into the Christian faith.

Every baptized person not yet confirmed can and should receive the sacrament of Confirmation. In the Western, or Latin, tradition the "age of discretion" is given as the expected age for receiving the sacrament. Children in danger of death should also be confirmed even if they have not attained the age of discretion (CCC, 1307).

This age is normally thought of as being "the age of reason," around seven years old. Local custom in many places has delayed Confirmation until a later age, with the result that it is celebrated after First Eucharist instead of before, as is the more ancient custom.

... Preparation for Confirmation ...

Preparation for Confirmation should help a person grow closer to Christ and become more familiar with the Holy Spirit as present today through the gifts of the Holy Spirit. The preparation should awaken within the person a sense of belonging to the Church of Jesus Christ as both a universal Church and a parish community. This sense of belonging is strengthened by the support the person receives during the preparation process. It in turn heightens the person's awareness that their parish is not only a place of worship but a place where the faith of the person is nourished and is lived.

..... Sponsor for Confirmation .....

A sponsor, who is a fully initiated Catholic, is chosen for the sacrament of Confirmation. The sponsor may be the godparent who was present at Baptism. This provides unity between the two

Why is Confirmation celebrated after Baptism in the Western Churches and at the same time as Baptism in the Eastern Churches?

(CCC, 1290–1292)

In the Western Churches, the bishop had to be present in order to confirm. As the practice of baptizing infants became more common and the number of dioceses and rural parishes grew, it became impossible for him to perform both Baptism and Confirmation. This caused a separation between the celebration of the two sacraments. The priest was able to baptize the infants, and later the bishop would confirm those who had been baptized.

In the East, the priest baptizes and confirms the infant with "myron," consecrated by the bishop. This practice emphasizes the unity of Christian initiation, while the Western Churches emphasize the unity and communion with the bishop who is servant of the "one, holy, catholic, and apostolic church." It is the adult cate-chumen in the Western Churches who receives all three Sacraments of Initiation at the same time.

.... Discuss:

How does each way of celebrating the sacrament of Confirmation bring out the fuller meaning of the sacrament?

sacraments. This sponsor is usually a role model of faith who does and will continue to support and inspire the person to be confirmed in growing in and living their faith.

.... Confirmation Name ....

A confirmation name is sometimes chosen to remind the person of their baptism, when they received their first Christian name as a new creation and member of the Body of Christ. Usually a saint's name is chosen to inspire the person in their life as a Christian.

The Minister of Confirmation

The original minister of Confirmation is the bishop. In the Eastern Churches the priest who baptizes also immediately confirms the person as well. In the Western, or Latin, Churches, the law gives permission to confirm to priests:

❑ when they baptize adults or school-age children, and

❑ when they receive a person baptized into another Christian denomination into the full communion of the Catholic Church.

Although the bishop is the ordinary minister of Confirmation, under certain circumstances he may give priests the faculty of administering Confirmation in situations other than those mentioned above.

The Effects of Confirmation

From the first Christians in Jerusalem until now and the end of time, the sacraments celebrate, and make us sharers in, the Paschal mystery of Christ. This mystery is so rich that each sacrament celebrates it in its own unique way. "There are *sacramental graces,* gifts proper to the different sacraments" (CCC, 2003).

The Pentecost story reveals to us the primary grace, or effect, of the sacrament of Confirmation—the full outpouring of the Holy Spirit. "Confirmation brings an increase and deepening of baptismal grace:

❏ it roots us more deeply in the divine filiation which makes us cry, 'Abba! Father!' (Romans 8:15);

❏ it unites us more firmly to Christ;

❏ it increases the gifts of the Holy Spirit in us;

❏ it renders our bond with the Church more perfect (see *Constitution on the Church,* 11);

❏ it gives us a special strength of the Holy Spirit to spread and defend the faith by word and action as true witnesses of Christ, to confess the name of Christ boldly, and never to be ashamed of the Cross (see Council of Florence [1439] DS 1319; *Constitution on the Church,* 11; 12)" (CCC, 1303).

This epiclesis prayer, which the bishop or priest-celebrant prays in the celebration of Confirmation in the Roman Rite, helps us gain a better understanding of our reception of Confirmation.

Preparing for Confirmation

Think about your own preparation for Confirmation. In what ways did it help you?

Think about your celebration of Confirmation. How has it changed your relation to Christ? To the Church?

Looking back at your own experiences, suggest ideas that you think should be included in the confirmation preparation process. Give your reasons for including each.

Suggestions   **Reasons**

Extending his hands over those to be confirmed, he prays:

> All-powerful God, Father of our Lord
>   Jesus Christ,
> by water and the Holy Spirit
> you freed your sons and daughters
>   from sin
> and gave them new life.
> Send your Holy Spirit upon them
> to be their Helper and Guide.
> Give them the spirit of wisdom and
>   understanding,
> the spirit of right judgment and
>   courage,
> the spirit of knowledge and
>   reverence.
> Fill them with the spirit of wonder
>   and awe in your presence.
> We ask this through Christ our Lord.
>   Amen.

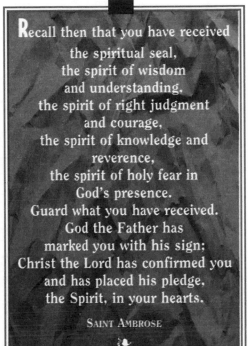

Recall then that you have received
the spiritual seal,
the spirit of wisdom
and understanding,
the spirit of right judgment
and courage,
the spirit of knowledge and
reverence,
the spirit of holy fear in
God's presence.
Guard what you have received.
God the Father has
marked you with his sign;
Christ the Lord has confirmed you
and has placed his pledge,
the Spirit, in your hearts.

SAINT AMBROSE

Relief of *Pentecost*.
Titian (1488–1576)

Prayer

❖ ❖ ❖

The epiclesis prayer, which is prayed at the consecration of the chrism, or myron. is from the Syriac liturgy of Antioch.

> **[Father . . . send your Holy**
> **Spirit] on us**
> **and on this oil which is before**
> **us**
> **and consecrate it,**
> **so that it may be for all who are**
> **anointed**
> **and marked with it holy myron,**
> **priestly myron, royal myron,**
> **anointing with gladness,**
> **clothing with light,**
> **a cloak of salvation,**
> **a spiritual gift,**
> **the sanctification of souls and**
> **bodies, imperishable**
> **happiness,**
> **the indelible seal,**
> **a buckler of faith,**
> **and a fearsome helmet against**
> **all the works of the adversary.**

REVIEW

IMPORTANT TERMS TO KNOW

chrism—the blessed, scented oil used in the sacrament of Confirmation; it is also used in Baptism and Holy Orders.

chrismation—the name given to Confirmation in the Eastern Churches, referring to the chrism and anointing with chrism that is consecrated by the bishop

Christ—the Greek word for "Anointed One," given to Jesus

Confirmation—Sacrament of Initiation in which we celebrate the special gift of the Holy Spirit; the sacrament that completes the sacrament of Baptism

Messiah—the Hebrew word for "Anointed One," given to Jesus

myron—a word used for chrism and chrismation in the liturgy of the Eastern Churches

Pentecost—refers to the coming of the Holy Spirit upon the disciples

CHAPTER SUMMARY

Confirmation completes Baptism and continues our initiation into the Church. In this chapter we learned:

1. The confirmed are perfectly bound to the Church and are sealed with the gift of the Holy Spirit.

2. Christian Scriptures refer to the Holy Spirit present at the baptism of Jesus, descending upon the disciples at Pentecost, and on new Christians at Baptism.

3. The whole life and mission of Jesus was lived out in union with the Holy Spirit given to him by the Father in abundant measure.

4. The anointing with chrism and the laying on of hands while saying the words "Be sealed with the gift of the Holy Spirit" are the essential elements of the Rite of Confirmation (CCC, 1320).

5. The sacrament of Confirmation, as Baptism does, marks the person with an indelible character that seals the person with the Holy Spirit. This sacrament is received only once.

6. Any baptized person not yet confirmed can receive Confirmation. In the Roman Rite the bishop is the original and ordinary minister of Confirmation.

7. The effects of Confirmation are a full outpouring of the Holy Spirit and increased baptismal grace, uniting us firmly to Christ, with strength to spread and defend the faith by word and action.

EXPLORING OUR CATHOLIC FAITH

1. Listening to the Word of God

Jesus proclaimed that the words of Isaiah are fulfilled in him. Read and reflect on Luke 4:18–19. Explain how we as Christians can fulfill the works of one who was "anointed" by the Spirit.

2. Understanding the Teachings of the Catholic Church

The Second Vatican Council taught that the baptized are "more perfectly bound to the Church and are endowed with the special strength of the Holy Spirit" and "are, as true witnesses of Christ, more strictly obliged to spread the faith by word and deed" (*Constitution on the Church,* 11). Explain your understanding of this teaching, using the rites of the anointing of oil with the laying on of hands.

3. Reflecting on Our Catholic Faith

Saint Cyril of Alexandria, who was bishop of Alexandria from 412 to 444, wrote: "It can easily be shown from examples both in the Old Testament and the New that the Spirit changes those in whom he comes to dwell; he so transforms them that they begin to live a completely new kind of life." Reflect on this insight of Saint Cyril. In what ways does it speak about your life? Write your reflections in your journal.

4. Living Our Catholic Faith

You have been anointed with the Spirit. Discuss ways that you are spreading the faith. Brainstorm new ways you can spread faith in Christ.

CHAPTER 6

Eucharist

"Amen, amen, I say to you, unless you eat the flesh of the Son of Man and drink his blood, you do not have life within you."

JOHN 6:53

What Do You Think?

Tell why you agree or disagree with this statement: Catholics and Protestants believe exactly the same thing when they say the bread and wine become the Body and Blood of Jesus.

Several years ago the film *Babette's Feast* won the Academy Award for best film. It is about a very traditional, religious family that hires a woman to be their cook. Little does the family know that the woman they have hired is actually a gourmet cook who is without employment. After winning the lottery, the cook proceeds to use the money to make a gourmet feast in appreciation to the family.

When the family and friends gather around the table, they bring with them all of their past grudges, resentments, and disagreements. No one talks except to bring up unforgotten problems and hurts. Gradually, as they begin sharing the meal, it transforms the family, and reconciliation and forgiveness of past sins begin to take place.

What are some important meals in your life? Has sharing a meal with others ever had a big significance in your life? Explain.

KEY TERMS

anaphora

Blessed Sacrament

breaking of the bread

Eucharist

Mass

synaxis

transubstantiation

viaticum

A scene from *Babette's Feast*, a film by Gabriel Axel, © 1988 Orion Pictures Corporation.

The deeper meaning of sharing a meal is the fulcrum of this wonderful, highly recommended movie. A meal and fellowship lead family members to be reconciled with one another. Past hurts are healed; broken relationships are reconciled; new life is celebrated. In some ways, reflecting on this film helps us understand what happens when we gather for the celebration of the Eucharist. In this chapter we will explore the meaning of the Eucharist—the meaning of its words and symbolic actions for our lives as members of the Body of Christ.

(Catechism of the Catholic Church, 1328–1334)

The Eucharist: The Source and Summit of the Life of the Church

The **Eucharist** completes Christian initiation. The newly baptized Christians join with the community of the faithful at the table of the Lord. They now share in the Eucharist, the "source and summit of the Christian life" (*Constitution on the Church*, 11), with which all other sacraments and church ministries are bound up and toward which all are oriented.

The Institution of the Eucharist

The institution of the Eucharist refers to the actual event of the Last Supper at which Jesus gave us the Eucharist:

In order to leave them a pledge of this love, in order never to depart from his own and to make them sharers in his Passover, he instituted

---

What the Documents Say

The Church and the world have a great need for Eucharistic worship. Jesus awaits us in this sacrament of love. Let us not refuse the time to go to meet him in adoration, in contemplation full of faith, and open to making amends for the serious offenses and crimes of the world. Let our adoration never cease (John Paul II, *Mystery and Worship of the Eucharist*, 3).

.... Discuss:

Compare the teachings of Pope John Paul II with your understanding of *Babette's Feast*. In what ways does the conversion of the characters in the film give you insight into the meaning of the Eucharist?

the Eucharist as the memorial of his death and Resurrection, and commanded his apostles to celebrate it until his return. CCC, 1337

This memorial meal of the Lord's Passover, of his passion and resurrection, is at the center of the Church's life.

The Eucharist is the heart and the summit of the Church's life, for in it Christ associates his Church and all her members with his sacrifice of praise and thanksgiving offered once for all on the cross to his Father; by this sacrifice he pours out the graces of salvation on his Body which is the Church. CCC, 1407

The Many Names of the Sacrament

Christian tradition has given many names to our celebration of the Lord's Supper. Each, in its own way, helps us penetrate some aspect of this great mystery of our faith.

Eucharist. The Greek words *eucharistein* and *eulogein* mean "to bless" and "to give thanks." Both words "recall the Jewish blessings that proclaim—especially during a meal—God's works: creation, redemption, and sanctification" (CCC, 1328).

The Lord's Supper. On Holy Thursday evening, we gather to celebrate the Mass of the Lord's Supper. This name, Lord's Supper, points to the connection between the Eucharist and the Last Supper. It passes on to us the belief of the Church that when we gather to celebrate the Eucharist we are fulfilling Jesus' command to "Do this in remembrance of me" (1 Corinthians 11:24).

The Eucharist also anticipates the meal that Jesus will share with all the blessed in the kingdom—the wedding feast of the Lamb in the heavenly Jerusalem (Revelation 19:9).

Breaking of the Bread. **Breaking of the bread** is central to the Christian story. It came to be the first image the Christians used to describe the gathering of the community for the Eucharist (Acts of the Apostles 2:42).

At the Eucharist we are and form the one Body of Christ. We are made one with him and with one another. The expression "breaking of the bread" was used by the first Christians to profess that belief (1 Corinthians 10:16–17).

Jesus not only broke bread, blessed it, and shared it at the Last Supper; he also does so in the gospel story of the multiplication of the loaves and fishes (Matthew 14:19, 15:36; Mark 8:6, 19). It is also in the breaking of the bread that the disciples in the Emmaus story (Luke 24:30–31) come to recognize the risen Jesus.

Synaxis (Eucharistic Assembly). The Greek word for "gathered assembly" is **synaxis.** The assembly celebrates the Eucharist as a visible expression of the Church. The whole Church, the Body of Christ, Head and members, join as one in blessing and giving thanks to the Father.

Memorial. The Eucharist is the memorial of Christ's Paschal mystery. When the Church celebrates the Eucharist, Christ's Paschal mystery "is made present: the sacrifice Christ offered once for all on the cross remains ever present (Hebrews 7:25–27)" (CCC, 1364). Summarizing this faith, the Church teaches:

As often as the sacrifice of the cross by which "Christ our Pasch is sacrificed" (1 Corinthians 5:7) is celebrated on the altar, the work of our redemption is carried out.

Dogmatic Constitution on the Church, 3

Blessing and Thanking God

The word *eucharist* means, first of all, "thanksgiving." List some things for which you are grateful or thankful.

.... Discuss:

What do you do to show your gratitude for these things? What does this show others about your relationship with God?

The Holy Sacrifice. The Eucharist makes present the sacrifice of Christ and enables us to share in it. "The lives of the faithful, their praise, sufferings, prayer, and work, are united with those of Christ and with his total offering, and so acquire a new value" (CCC, 1368).

The expressions *"sacrifice of praise"* (Hebrews 13:15), *"spiritual sacrifices"* (1 Peter 2:5), *"sacrifice of thanksgiving"* (Psalm 116:17), and *pure and holy sacrifice* (Malachi 1:11) are also used. These terms help express our belief that Christ's sacrifice "completes and surpasses all the sacrifices of the Old Covenant" (CCC, 1330).

The Holy and Divine Liturgy and **Sacred Mysteries.** The Eucharist is the most intense expression of our faith. All other sacraments and ministries are linked with the Eucharist and directed toward it.

Most Blessed Sacrament. The term *Most Blessed Sacrament* refers to the eucharistic species, the consecrated bread reserved in the tabernacle. The primary purpose of reserving the eucharistic species outside Mass is the administration of **viaticum.** Other reasons are bringing Communion to the sick and the adoration of the Lord present in the Eucharist.

Holy Communion. The name *Holy Communion* expresses our belief that sharing in the Eucharist unites us to Christ and to all the faithful.

The Holy Mass. The name Holy **Mass** calls our attention to our belief that the Eucharist nourishes us to live our life in Christ. The root of the English word *mass* is the Latin word *missa*, "sent."

The Rite of the Eucharist

The mystery of the Eucharist is the true center of the sacred liturgy and of the whole Christian life. "The Eucharistic celebration always includes: the proclamation of the Word of God; thanksgiving to God the Father for all his benefits, above all the gift of his Son; the consecration of bread and wine; and participation in the liturgical banquet by receiving the Lord's body and blood. These elements constitute one single act of worship" (CCC, 1408).

The Liturgical Celebration of the Eucharist

Christ himself presides over every eucharistic celebration. It is in his name that we come together to join with him to bless and give thanks to the Father.

Each one of us has a part to play in the celebration. The priest or bishop "acting in the person of Christ, the Head" presides over and leads the assembly in prayer. Together, we should "become one body, whether by hearing the word of God, joining in prayers and song, or above all by offering the sacrifice together and sharing together in the Lord's table" (*Roman Missal*, General Instruction, 62).

Gathering (Introductory Rites)

The purpose of these rites is to have the faithful form one community and prepare themselves to listen to God's Word and celebrate the Eucharist properly.

Liturgy of the Word

God speaks to us through the proclamation of the Word. This proclamation includes readings from both the Old Testament and the New Testament.

The homily, after the readings, helps us understand and live out in our lives today the Word of God that has just been proclaimed. After the homily, we express our beliefs in the Nicene Creed. In the intercessions, or prayers of the faithful, we pray for the needs of the Church and all people.

Liturgy of the Eucharist

Only validly ordained priests can preside at the Eucharist and consecrate the bread and wine that become the Body and Blood of Christ. The essential elements of this sacrament are:

- ❏ bread and wine in the form of wheat bread and grape wine,
- ❏ the power of the Holy Spirit invoked over the bread and wine, and
- ❏ the words spoken by Jesus at the Last Supper, repeated by the priest.

Preparation of the Gifts and Altar. We begin the Liturgy of the Eucharist with the preparation of the gifts and altar. Traditionally, a collection of money or food was also taken at this time to help those in need and presented with the gifts of bread and wine.

Anaphora. The **anaphora,** or eucharistic prayer, is next. This includes the prayer of thanksgiving and the words of institution. The epiclesis and anamnesis are also prayed. The Holy Spirit is invoked to make the bread and wine into the Body and Blood of Jesus and to make present once again the memorial of the death and resurrection of Jesus in our midst.

Communion Rite. We pray the Lord's Prayer and exchange the sign of peace to prepare to receive Holy Communion. The breaking of the bread takes place and the bread is distributed among those gathered together.

Concluding Rite
··········(Dismissal)··········

We are sent forth with the command: "The Mass is ended, go in peace." We are to seek to do God's will in our daily lives. We are to live as Jesus' disciples and announce the Good News.

Q&A

Do we receive the Body and Blood of Jesus when we only receive the bread without the wine?
CCC, 1390

"Since Christ is sacramentally present under each of the species, communion under the species of bread alone makes it possible to receive all the fruit of Eucharistic grace." However, " 'the sign of communion is more complete when given under both kinds, since in that form the sign of the Eucharistic meal appears more clearly' " (*Roman Missal, General Instruction,* 240).

It is desirable that, whenever possible, we receive Communion under the fuller sign of both species. We eat the bread and drink from the cup as Jesus did with his disciples.

(CCC, 1333–1336, 1356–1361, 1382–1390, 1391–1398, 1402–1405)

Understanding the Mystery

When Jesus told his disciples that his flesh and blood were food and drink, his listeners reacted to his words with doubt and confusion.

> Then many of his disciples who were listening said, "This saying is hard; who can accept it?"
> **John 6:60**

The reality Jesus was revealing was a mystery. We have come to believe and have deepened our faith in the Eucharist. Here are some of the dimensions of this great mystery that help us probe its meaning.

Sacramental Sacrifice

The "sacrifice of the cross and its sacramental renewal in the Mass . . . are one and the same, differing only in manner of offering" (*Roman Missal,* General Instruction, 2).

Sacrifice of Thanksgiving and Praise. In the Eucharist we present to the Father the whole of creation. We bless and give thanksgiving and praise to the Father, who is the source and giver of all blessings. The good things of the earth represented by the bread and wine, which God has made, are given back to God to be made holy, as we are holy.

Sacrificial Memorial. The sacrifice is not just an event from the past that is remembered. It is an event brought into the present, by the power of the Holy Spirit. The words of institution are words of sacrifice. We unite our suffering, in the day-to-day struggles of life, with the sufferings of Christ.

The sacrifice we offer is more than an offering of bread and wine. It is truly the Body and Blood of Christ that we offer. *Transubstantiation* is the term we use to describe the change of bread and wine into the Body and Blood of Christ.

Presence of Christ. Christ Jesus is present with us in many ways. He himself told us that he is present with us whenever two or three of his followers gather in his name (Matthew 18:20); he is also present in people who are living in poverty, imprisoned, or suffering (Matthew 25:31–46).

When we gather to give thanks and praise to God for all that we have received, we encounter Christ, present with us. First, he is always present in the assembly gathered in his name. Second, he is present in his Word, speaking to us through the Scripture proclaimed in the liturgy. Third, he is present in the priest, "the same now offering through the ministry of the priest who formerly offered himself on

Participating in the Celebration of the Eucharist

Statistics reveal that more than half of baptized Catholics stays home on Sunday. List the reasons you hear people give to tell why they do not attend the Eucharist on any given Sunday.

 Discuss:

Write an appropriate response to each of the reasons listed.

the cross" (Council of Trent). Above all we believe "he is present . . . but especially in the Eucharistic species" (*Constitution on the Sacred Liturgy,* 7).

> Under the consecrated species of bread and wine Christ himself, living and glorious, is present in a true, real, and substantial manner: his Body and his Blood, with his soul and his divinity.   CCC, 1413

The Paschal Banquet

To receive Communion is to receive Christ himself, who has offered himself for us: "[T]he celebration of the Eucharistic sacrifice is wholly directed toward the intimate union of the faithful with Christ through communion" (CCC, 1382).

The Table of the Lord. The altar as a symbol helps us understand two dimensions of the Eucharist—the altar of sacrifice and the table of the Lord. It is the table on which the Lord's Supper is set. We adore this sacrament because it is the sacred food, the Body and Blood of Christ, we receive unto life eternal.

Communion. We take part most fully in the celebration of the Eucharist through sacramental Communion. It is "strongly recommended that we receive it during Mass" (*Instruction on the Worship of the Eucharistic Mystery,* 31). By sharing in and receiving the Body and Blood of Christ, we become one and strengthen our unity, our "communion," as the Body of Christ. Sharing in the Eucharist is the source of sharing in, or having communion with, the very life of God.

The Church invites us to take Jesus' invitation seriously. We are asked to take part in the celebration of the Eucharist every Sunday and on holy days of obligation. We are required actually to receive Holy Communion at least once a year during the Easter season.

To accept this invitation demands that we prepare ourselves properly. We prepare ourselves during the celebration of the Eucharist. First, in the penitential rite, we praise God for his mercy, asking his forgiveness for any sins we have committed. During the communion rite, we share a sign of peace with our neighbor, and then, just before Communion, we say the words of the centurion: "Lord, I am not worthy to have you enter under my roof; only say the word and my servant will be healed" (Matthew 8:8).

We also must prepare ourselves before we gather. We prepare by celebrating the sacrament of Penance if we have committed a grave and serious sin.

> Anyone who desires to receive Christ in Eucharistic communion must be in the state of grace. Anyone aware of having sinned mortally must not receive communion without having received absolution in the sacrament of penance.   CCC, 1415

Fasting before the Eucharist is also a tradition in our Church. By fasting, or not eating, we purify our minds and hearts and focus our attention on our relationship with God and others.

. . . . Fruits of Communion . . . .

Just as the names given to the sacrament of the Eucharist are many, so are the fruits of the sacrament. The first fruit, or grace, is our intimate union with Christ.

Eucharistic communion separates us from sin. Jesus died for us and shed his blood for the forgiveness of our sins. By our participation in the Eucharist our venial sins are forgiven and we are strengthened against grave sins.

The Eucharist strengthens us for living the Great Commandment to love God and others as we love ourselves. To receive the Real Presence of Christ in the bread and wine we must also recognize the real presence of Jesus in the poorest of the poor around us.

The Eucharist also deepens the unity of the Church as the mystical Body of Christ. At Baptism we become members of the Body of Christ. It is the Eucharist that reinforces that unity. The Eucharist also invites unity among all Christians.

We recognize that the Eastern Churches have preserved apostolic succession and so possess the sacraments of Holy Orders and the Eucharist. Under certain circumstances, with the permission of the local bishop, receiving the Eucharist with Eastern Christians is not only possible but also encouraged.

Our Protestant brothers and sisters " 'have not preserved the proper reality of the Eucharistic mystery in its fullness, especially because of the absence of the sacrament of Holy Orders (*Decree on Ecumenism*, 22§3).' It is for this reason that Eucharistic intercommunion with these communities is not possible for the Catholic Church" (CCC, 1400).

Pledge of Future Glory

At the Last Supper, Jesus promised:

> "I tell you, from now on I shall not drink this fruit of the vine until the day when I drink it with you new in the kingdom of my Father." **Matthew 26:29**

While we live on this earth, we are in a process of waiting for the fullness of the kingdom of God to come. We believe and hope that we will see Christ still more clearly when he comes again in glory and we join him at the heavenly banquet.

The Eucharist is our pledge, or promise, of this future glory.

READING THE BIBLE

Look up the following Scripture passages. Describe each passage and explain how it prefigures the Eucharist we celebrate today.

Genesis 14:18–20

Deuteronomy 8:2–3

Exodus 12:17

Matthew 14:13–21, 15:32–38

Prayer

❖ ❖ ❖

The Pange Lingua is a masterpiece of medieval poetry written by Thomas Aquinas around 1264. The last stanza is the hymn traditionally sung at the Benediction of the Blessed Sacrament.

Pange Lingua

Hail our Savior's glorious Body,
Which his Virgin Mother bore;
Hail the Blood which, shed
   for sinners,
Did a broken world restore;
Hail the sacrament most holy,
Flesh and Blood of Christ adore!

Come, adore this wondrous
   presence;
Bow to Christ, the source of grace!
Here is kept the ancient promise
Of God's earthly dwelling-place!
Sight is blind before God's glory,
Faith alone may see his face!

Glory be to God the Father,
Praise to his coequal Son,
Adoration to the Spirit,
Bond of love, in Godhead one!
Blest be God by all creation
Joyously while ages run!

REVIEW

IMPORTANT TERMS TO KNOW

anaphora—the Greek word that refers to the eucharistic prayer

Blessed Sacrament—the Body and Blood of Jesus, kept, or reserved, in the tabernacle

breaking of the bread—the name the early gathering of the Christians used for the Eucharist

Eucharist—Sacrament of Initiation in which we share in the Paschal mystery of Christ and receive the Body and Blood of Christ, who is truly and really present under the appearances of bread and wine

Mass—from the Latin term *missa*, which refers to the dismissal of the faithful to fulfill God's will in their daily lives

synaxis—the Greek word referring to the gathering of the Christian community as the Body of Christ at the Eucharist

transubstantiation—refers to the change that occurs when the bread and wine become the Body and Blood of Christ

viaticum—name for Holy Communion when it is given to the dying; in Latin it means "food for the journey."

CHAPTER SUMMARY

The sacrament of the Eucharist completes the initiation of the newly baptized into full communion with the Church, the Body of Christ. In this chapter we learned:

1. The Eucharist is the source and summit of the Christian life.

2. The institution of the Eucharist took place at the Last Supper. Jesus took bread and wine and said it was his body and blood to eat and drink. He commanded the disciples, "Do this in remembrance of me" (1 Corinthians 11:24).

3. The celebration of the Eucharist has two main parts: the Liturgy of the Word and the Liturgy of the Eucharist. Together they form one single act of worship.

4. The essential elements of the rite consist of bread and wine, the invocation of the Holy Spirit upon the bread and wine, and the words of consecration spoken by Jesus at the Last Supper that are repeated by a validly ordained priest.

5. The Eucharist is a sacramental sacrifice. It is a reminder of the heavenly banquet that we will celebrate after our life here on earth, when we will join with all of the faithful departed around the heavenly table.

6. We are to be properly prepared for the Eucharist.

7. The Church invites us to celebrate the Eucharist every Sunday and on holy days of obligation, and to receive the Eucharist at least once a year at Easter.

8. The fruits of the Eucharist are increased union with Christ, unity as the Body of Christ, and forgiveness of venial sins.

EXPLORING OUR CATHOLIC FAITH

1. Listening to God's Word

Saint Paul wrote, "Because the loaf of bread is one, we, though many, are one body, for we all partake of the one loaf" (1 Corinthians 10:17). What does this truth about the Eucharist say to you about your relationship with God? With others?

2. Understanding the Teachings of the Catholic Church

The Eucharist is spiritual food and drink: "What the faithful have received by faith and sacrament in the celebration of the Eucharist should have its effect on their way of life" (*Instruction on the Worship of the Eucharistic Mystery*, 13). What effects does taking part in the celebration of the Eucharist have on your life?

3. Reflecting on Our Catholic Faith

Saint Irenaeus (130–202), who was a bishop and martyr, wrote: "Our way of thinking is attuned to the Eucharist, and the Eucharist in turn confirms our way of thinking" (*Against Heresy*). Reflect on this insight of faith. What does it say to you about your participation in the Eucharist? Write your reflections in your journal.

4. Living Our Catholic Faith

After each celebration of the Eucharist, we are sent forth with the command, "Go in peace to love and serve the Lord." Brainstorm ways you can put that command into practice.

CHAPTER 7

Penance

"Whose sins you forgive are forgiven them,
and whose sins you retain are retained."

JOHN 20:23

Write "T" next to the statements that are true, "F" next to those that are false, and "N" next to those that you are uncertain about. Share your responses, giving reasons for each choice.

_____ 1. The sacrament of Penance is only celebrated once in a person's life.

_____ 2. Sin disrupts our relationship with God and with the Church.

_____ 3. Jesus gave his apostles authority to forgive sins.

_____ 4. Three forms of doing penance are prayer, fasting, and almsgiving.

In Victor Hugo's book *Les Miserables* there is a classic story of forgiveness and reconciliation. Jean Valjean spends nineteen years in prison for stealing a loaf of bread to feed his starving sister's baby. Upon his release from prison, Valjean cannot find anyone to give him shelter because he has the look of a convict. A kind bishop invites him to stay at his house for the night, and Jean Valjean repays the bishop by stealing his silverware. The police catch him soon afterward, and Valjean is brought before the bishop with the silverware.

Instead of having Valjean arrested, the bishop tells the police that he gave the silverware to Valjean, adding that Valjean had forgotten two other silver candlesticks that were also given to him. The police leave in a state of shock and confusion, while Jean Valjean is left standing free and forgiven before the bishop.

When has someone forgiven you for a big mistake you made? How did you feel after that? How did it change your life?

KEY TERMS

absolution

confession

contrition

conversion

excommunication

sacrament of Penance

sacramental seal

sin

The bishop's act of forgiveness is so powerful that Jean Valjean starts a new life—changing his ways to make the world a better place. The silver candlesticks become a constant reminder of the bishop's kindness and forgiveness. In this chapter we will begin our study of the Church's two Sacraments of Healing: the sacrament of Penance and the sacrament of the Anointing of the Sick. This chapter will focus on Penance and Reconciliation.

(Catechism of the Catholic Church, 1423–1424)

The Mystery of God's Forgiveness

Each day the Spirit invites us to live our lives as Christians. Yet each day we experience people or events that tempt us to turn away from God. We experience the temptation to sin.

Jesus' Ministry of Forgiveness

Jesus reached out to sinners and invited them to trust in and accept the loving forgiveness of his Father. To the woman whom the scribes and Pharisees freely were willing to condemn, Jesus said:

> "Woman, where are they? Has no one condemned you?" She replied, "No one, sir." Then Jesus said, "Neither do I condemn you. Go, [and] from now on do not sin any more."
> **John 8:10–11**

Only God forgives sins. Jesus, throughout his ministry, not only preached about God's forgiving, reconciling love, but also forgave sins. His Paschal mystery—his death-resurrection—fulfilled and brought about God's plan of salvation and redemption, God's plan of forgiveness.

In the gospel story of the healing of the paralytic, the scribes strongly objected in their hearts when Jesus forgave the paralytic. They accused him of blaspheming, of claiming to do only what God can do—forgive sins.

> Jesus immediately knew in his mind what they were thinking to themselves, so he said, "Why are you thinking such things in your hearts? Which is easier, to say to the paralytic, 'Your sins are forgiven,' or to say, 'Rise, pick up your mat and walk'? But that you may know that the Son of Man has authority to forgive sins on earth"—he said to the paralytic, "I say to you, rise, pick up your mat, and go home." He rose, picked up his mat at once, and went away in the sight of everyone.
> **Mark 2:8–12**

Jesus welcomed sinners back into the community of the People of God. He ate with sinners, which was scandalous and outrageous behavior to the religious authorities of his day. He welcomed the penitent woman into his presence to the chagrin of Simon the Pharisee and his guests. He preached about the lost coin, the lost sheep, and the lost son. He revealed that God is actively present with us, calling us to return when we are "lost."

When his work on earth was completed, Jesus shared this ministry of forgiveness with his apostles. He gave this authority to others to exercise in his name (John 20:21–23).

The entire Church, the Body of Christ in the world, is to be a sign and instrument of God's forgiving, reconciling love. But the power to absolve sins "in the name of the Father, and of the Son, and of the holy Spirit" has been given to the apostles and those who have succeeded them. When Jesus gave Peter the keys to the kingdom of heaven, he said:

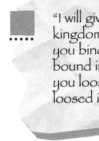

> "I will give you the keys to the kingdom of heaven. Whatever you bind on earth shall be bound in heaven; and whatever you loose on earth shall be loosed in heaven."
>
> **Matthew 16:19**

It is this authority—assigned to Peter and the successors of the apostles—that is shared by the bishops and priests of the Church, who are sent out as "ambassadors for Christ, as if God were appealing through us," and pleading, "[B]e reconciled to God" (2 Corinthians 5:20).

Jesus reveals God's joy when even one sinner trusts in him, turns to him, and accepts his mercy. He concludes the parable of the lost coin with this teaching:

> "In just the same way, I tell you, there will be rejoicing among the angels of God over one sinner who repents."
>
> **Luke 15:10**

READING THE BIBLE

Read and prayerfully reflect on these passages from the New Testament.

Luke 15:15–24 (The Parable of the Lost Son)

Acts 9:1–19 (Saul's Conversion)

Mark 2:1–12 (The Healing of a Paralytic)

Mark 2:13–17 (The Call of Levi)

.... Discuss:

In what ways is each

- A story of conversion?
- A story of reconciliation?
- A story of forgiveness?
- A story of healing?

Jesus' work of forgiveness and reconciliation culminated in his Paschal mystery. Through his death and resurrection, which he offered for all, we have been reconciled with God. "God was reconciling the world to himself in Christ," Paul taught. "For our sake he made him to be sin who did not know sin, so that we might become the righteousness of God in him" (2 Corinthians 5:19, 21).

(CCC, 1430–1449)

Penance and Reconciliation

"S in sets itself against God's love for us and turns our hearts away from it" (CCC, 1850). Sin is an offense against God that disrupts our communion with God the Father, Son, and Holy Spirit, and also our communion with the Church, the Body of Christ. The Church's **sacrament of Penance** celebrates and makes present among us the mystery of God's forgiving and reconciling love.

Living Lives of Penance

The dictionary defines *penance* as "a voluntary suffering or punishment to show repentance for wrongdoing." The Church has a rich tradition of penance, which helps us understand the mystery of **conversion** and forgiveness celebrated in the sacrament of Penance.

Forms of Penance

It is the Holy Spirit that brings our sins to light and gives us the grace for repentance and conversion.

> Interior repentance is a radical reorientation of our whole life, a return, a conversion to God with all our heart, an end of sin, a turning away from evil, with repugnance toward the evil actions we have committed. At the same time it entails the desire and resolution to change one's life, with hope in God's mercy and trust in the help of his grace. CCC, 1431

Our interior conversion—the conversion of our heart—leads to visible signs, gestures, and works of penance.

Interior conversion can be expressed through prayer, fasting, and almsgiving, and in many other ways; for example:

❑ reaching to people in need;
❑ defending justice and right;
❑ admitting one's faults to another;
❑ reading Sacred Scripture;
❑ praying the Liturgy of the Hours, the Our Father, and other prayers; and
❑ participating in the liturgical seasons and days of penance, especially Lent.

Fridays, in particular, in the Christian tradition, are days on which we remember the death of Jesus and the forgiveness of our sins. On Fridays we practice acts of penance like fasting, prayer, almsgiving, and serving our neighbor.

These and other acts of penance express our desire for God and lead to our reconciliation with God, neighbor, and ourselves. They move our spirit to conversion and repentance and

There are many stories of conversion in Sacred Scripture. One of the more powerful is that of Peter. After three times denying even knowing Jesus, he wept with sorrow, recalling that Jesus had predicted that he would do this. Read the gospel story of Peter's denial in Luke 22:31–34, 54–62.

.... Discuss:

What does Peter's story of sorrow and conversion say to you about your relationship with Jesus?

contribute to the forgiveness of our sins. They are signs of our willingness to take up our cross daily to follow Jesus.

The Need for the Sacrament

Through the Sacraments of Initiation we are fully incorporated into the Body of Christ. We are reborn in the waters of Baptism, are filled with the Holy Spirit in Confirmation, and, in the Eucharist, are nourished with the grace to live our life in Christ. Despite this we know we are human beings who are tempted to sin and indeed do sin. In the sacrament of Penance the sins we commit after Baptism are forgiven.

When we sin, we freely and deliberately choose evil instead of good. We choose to adopt attitudes and values that are not built on the Beatitudes and to act in ways not guided by the command-

ments. We are in need of conversion, forgiveness, and reconciliation.

Our conversion entails God's forgiveness and reconciliation with the Church. This forgiveness and reconciliation are celebrated and made present in our lives through the sacrament of Penance.

Names for the Sacrament

Throughout the tradition of the Church, many names and images have been used to express our faith in this great mystery of God's forgiveness.

The Sacrament of Conversion. Jesus' life, death, and resurrection is the source of our **conversion** and our reconciliation with God. Jesus began his public ministry proclaiming, " 'This is the time of fulfillment. The kingdom of God is at hand. Repent, and believe in the gospel' " (Mark 1:15).

Starting Over in My Life

Think about moments in your life when you had to start over. Was it easy or hard? Did you learn from the past?

Starting over . . .

____ at a new school

____ after a punishment

____ with new friends

____ after a mistake

____ with a new boyfriend or girlfriend

____ with a new course

____ in a new house or neighborhood

____ after a death

____ after an athletic loss

■ **.... Discuss:**

Compare the experiences you named above with the experience of conversion.

The Sacrament of Penance. The sinner's personal and ecclesial process of conversion, penance, and satisfaction is called the sacrament of Penance.

The Sacrament of Confession. The disclosure or **confession** of sins to the priest is called the sacrament of confession. It is also a confession of thanks and praise for God's love and mercy.

The Sacrament of Forgiveness. The priest says the words of **absolution** and God grants pardon of the sinner's sins and peace.

The Sacrament of Reconciliation. After the confession of sins, the sinner now experiences God's love and mercy and is reconciled with God and their neighbor.

The Conversion of the Baptized

It is in Baptism that we first celebrate our conversion, the forgiveness of all our sins (original and personal), and our reconciliation with God. We receive the Spirit and promise to live that life of conversion throughout our lives.

Should we fail or weaken in our resolution and efforts, the Spirit calls us to conversion and repentance. He leads us to recognize sin in our lives and to get our lives headed in the right direction. The Spirit calls us to turn back to God and seek God's forgiveness with a contrite, sorrowful heart; and to trust in the mercy and love of God.

Celebrating the Sacrament of Penance and Reconciliation

The Church exercises the ministry of the sacrament of Penance through bishops and priests. This sacrament can be celebrated individually with the priest or communally with other penitents. In cases of grave necessity, the local bishop can grant a celebration of Penance with general confession and general absolution.

The Essential Elements of the Sacrament

The first essential element of the sacrament of Penance is the actions of the person seeking conversion through the power and grace of the Holy Spirit. These are contrition, confession, and satisfaction. The second element is the intervention of the Church through the bishop and priests, who absolve sins in the name of Jesus Christ and determine the manner of satisfaction or penance.

.... The Actions of the Penitent ....

The three actions of the penitent involve contrition (repentance), confession, and satisfaction (or penance).

Contrition. Our **contrition** is a gift from God and a prompting of the Holy Spirit. In seeking reconciliation, we are to show contrition for the sins committed, reject the sin committed, and resolve not to sin again.

True contrition arises out of our faith in God. In talking about contrition, we distinguish between "perfect" contrition and "imperfect" contrition. Perfect contrition arises out of our love of God. It leads to a remittance of venial sins, and the forgiveness of mortal sins if there is a firm resolution to celebrate the sacrament of Penance as soon as possible.

Imperfect contrition arises out of the ugliness of sin and our fear of eternal damnation or other penalties. Imperfect contrition disposes us to obtain forgiveness in the sacrament of Penance. By itself, it does not obtain the forgiveness of grave sins.

Confession of Sins. The confession, or disclosure, of sins to the priest involves admitting guilt and taking responsibility for the sins we have committed. All grave sins that are remembered through an examination of conscience must be confessed. The "individual and integral confession of grave sins followed by absolution remains the only ordinary means of reconciliation with God and with the Church" (CCC, 1497). "The confession of venial faults, without being necessary in itself, is nevertheless strongly recommended by the Church" (CCC, 1493).

The minister of the sacrament has the responsibility not to reveal any of the information stated by the penitent. We call this the **sacramental seal.** Severe penalties can occur if this seal is broken. These include the removal of faculties to continue celebrating the sacrament.

Satisfaction. When we sin, we turn away from God's love. We fail to show our love for our neighbor. We disrupt (venial sin) or even break (mortal sin) our relationship with God. After we sin, we need to repair the damage done by our sin. We call this "making satisfaction."

History of the Sacrament

● ●

(CCC, 1447)

During the first centuries, persons who committed grave sins—for example, idolatry, murder, or adultery—participated in rigorous acts of discipline and penance. They would do public penance for their sins, often for years, before receiving Reconciliation. Not everyone was accepted into this "order of penitents," and sometimes Reconciliation occurred only once in a lifetime.

During the seventh century, Irish missionaries started to meet privately with penitents, who confessed their sins to them. Their penance was also to be something privately expressed and not in a public forum.

In our current practice of the celebration of the sacrament of Penance, we can meet privately with the priest and celebrate the sacrament. We can also gather with many penitents to celebrate the sacrament. When we celebrate Penance with others, we confess our sins and receive absolution individually.

■
.... Discuss:
In what ways is the sacrament of Penance celebrated by your parish community?

True conversion is completed by expiation for sins, by amendment of life, and also by rectifying injuries done.

Rite of Penance, Introduction, 6c

The penance imposed by the priest guides us in making satisfaction. Examples of satisfaction may involve saying prayers, doing one of the works of mercy, serving one's neighbor, performing a voluntary act of self-denial, returning stolen property, restoring the reputation of someone we have slandered, or paying compensation for injuries.

All penances, or acts of making satisfaction, help remedy the damage caused by the sin and restore the relationships weakened or broken by our sins.

.....The Actions of the Minister.....

Christ entrusted the ministry of forgiveness and reconciliation to the apostles. The bishop is the visible head of the Church. Bishops, who are the successors of the apostles, are principally responsible for the ministry of reconciliation. Priests receive the ministry upon being commissioned by the local bishop or their religious superior or the pope.

Absolution. The priest is to be the servant of God's forgiveness. He is to imitate the example of Jesus. The priest gives absolution in the name of Christ. Holding his hands extended over the penitent, he prays the formula for absolution:

> God, the Father of mercies,
> through the death and resurrection
>   of his Son
> has reconciled the world to himself
> and sent the Holy Spirit among us
> for the forgiveness of sins;
> through the ministry of the Church
> may God give you pardon and peace,
> and I absolve you from your sins
> in the name of the Father, and of
>   the Son,
> and of the Holy Spirit.

Certain grave sins may incur **excommunication,** which is the most severe penalty the Church can carry out. Excommunication, which is very rare, removes the opportunity to receive the sacraments and to participate in other church activities. Absolution in these cases can be granted only by the pope, the bishop involved in the situation, or assigned priests.

The Effects of the Sacrament

Celebrating the sacrament of Penance reconciles us with God and with the Church, and anticipates eternal life.

Reconciliation with God. The primary purpose and effect of this sacrament is reconciliation of our friendship with God. Trusting in such a reconciliation, the Spirit blesses us with the gifts of peace and serenity.

Reconciliation with the Church. Sin also damages or breaks up our communion with the Church. Reconciliation restores or repairs this communion. The entire Church—not only the individual penitent—is transformed, reestablished, and strengthened when we reconcile with God.

Sin has a double consequence: eternal punishment and temporal punishment. Grave sin makes us incapable of eternal life, which is the eternal punishment for sin. All sin, venial and grave, "entails an unhealthy attachment to creatures" (CCC, 1472) from which we need to be purified. Purification frees one from the "temporal punishment" of sin.

Forgiveness of sins in the sacrament of Penance frees us from the eternal punishment of sin. The temporal punishment remains. We need to be free of the "unhealthy attachment" to sin. This purification is achieved in many ways, for example, prayer, works of mercy, acts of penance, and indulgences. Through indulgences "the faithful can obtain remission of temporal punishment resulting from sin for themselves and also for the souls in Purgatory" (CCC, 1498).

Anticipation of the Day of Judgment. Conversion and the confession of one's sins prepare us for entrance into the heavenly kingdom. Celebrating this sacrament offers us the opportunity to choose life over the death of sin. It anticipates that day when we will be judged or held accountable for our actions on this earth.

Prayer

❖ ❖ ❖

A traditional prayer said after penitents confess their sins is the act of contrition. In this prayer sinners confess their sorrow, reject sin, and resolve to sin no more.

ACT OF CONTRITION

O my God, I am heartily sorry
   for having offended You.

And I detest all my sins because
   of Your just punishments,
   but most of all because they
   offend You, my God,

who are all-good and deserving
   of all my love.

I firmly resolve, with the help
   of Your grace,

to sin no more

and to avoid the near occasions
   of sin.

Amen.

RITE OF PENANCE

IMPORTANT TERMS TO KNOW

absolution—words and blessings of the priest prayed in the sacrament of Penance that show God forgives our sins

confession—telling our sins to the priest in the sacrament of Penance

contrition—sorrow expressed for sins committed, the rejection of the sin, and a resolution not to sin again

conversion—a word that means "to turn around"; the invitation of the Holy Spirit to turn completely toward God and away from sin and evil

excommunication—the most severe penalty the Church can carry out. It usually involves the inability to receive the sacraments unless the bishop or the pope gives absolution.

sacrament of Penance—the Sacrament of Healing in which we celebrate God's gift of forgiveness and our reconciliation with God and with others; also called the sacrament of Reconciliation

sacramental seal—refers to the responsibility of the minister not to reveal any of the information stated by the penitent

CHAPTER SUMMARY

The sacrament of Penance is one of the two Sacraments of Healing. In this chapter we learned:

1. The sacrament of Penance is also called a sacrament of conversion, of confession, and of forgiveness. The Holy Spirit gives us the grace for repentance and conversion.

2. After Baptism the sacrament of Penance forgives our sins and reconciles us with God and the Church.

3. Jesus gave the authority to forgive sins to his apostles. Bishops, who are the successors of the apostles, and priests exercise this authority in the Church today in the sacrament of Penance.

4. The essential elements of the rite are the actions of the penitent through contrition, confession, and satisfaction; and the intervention of the Church through the bishop and priests who absolve us from sins.

5. The spiritual effects of the sacrament of Penance are reconciliation with God; reconciliation with the Church; remission, at least in part, of temporal punishment resulting from sin; peace and serenity of conscience; spiritual consolation; an increase of grace to live our life in Christ; and anticipation of the Day of Judgment.

EXPLORING OUR CATHOLIC FAITH

1. Listening to God's Word

In Romans 6:23, Saint Paul says that "the wages of sin is death, but the gift of God is eternal life in Christ Jesus our Lord." Describe what you think Paul means by "the wages of sin is death."

2. Understanding the Teachings of the Catholic Church

The introduction to the *Rite of Penance* says: "Jesus, however, not only exhorted people to repentance so that they would abandon their sins and turn wholeheartedly to the Lord, but welcoming sinners, he actually reconciled them with the Father." What does this tell us about who Jesus is?

3. Reflecting on Our Catholic Faith

Pope Clement I (92?–101) wrote, "Love unites us to God; it cancels innumerable sins, has no limits to its endurance, bears everything patiently." How does this quote help you understand the healing forgiveness of God? Write your thoughts in your journal.

4. Living Our Catholic Faith

Think of someone who is in need of healing or forgiveness. Call or visit them and offer your words of comfort and healing to them.

CHAPTER 8

Anointing of the Sick

[T]he prayer of faith will save the sick person,
and the Lord will raise him up.

JAMES 5:15

What Do You Think?

Do you agree or disagree with the statement "A person must be close to death in order to receive the sacrament of the **Anointing of the Sick**"?

List the reasons for your response.

Every night on national TV, we view people suffering throughout the world. The Catholic Church has always been a world-wide leader in reaching out to people who are poor and suffering throughout the world. Established in 1943, Catholic Relief Services is the official overseas relief and development agency of the Catholic bishops of the United States. Today Catholic Relief Services works in over eighty countries around the world, helping people on the basis of need—not creed, race, or nationality. The policies of the Catholic Relief Services continue the healing ministry of Jesus Christ among the poorest of the poor. Their mission is to alleviate human suffering, to aid in the development of people, and to foster charity and justice in the world.

What do you know about the relief efforts of the Church? Think about ways the three-fold mission of the Catholic Relief Services carries out the mission of the Church.

Sickness, suffering, and death are universal human experiences. Everyone has a personal story or a family story of illness that has in some way affected their life. Since its beginning the Church has addressed the mystery of suffering, has reflected on its meaning, and has reached out to those who suffer. In this chapter we will explore the second of the Church's Sacraments of Healing, the sacrament of the Anointing of the Sick.

(Catechism of the Catholic Church, 1500–1510)

Sickness and Healing

We are all troubled by suffering, illness, and death. The pain of these experiences is sometimes so overwhelming that some people may be tempted to doubt or even deny their faith and trust in God. Sacred Scripture passes on to us such stories. But in the midst of our suffering God makes himself known: "I, the LORD, am your healer" (Exodus 15:26). The Spirit invites us to strengthen our faith and trust in the Father's presence and love for us.

The Old Testament

The people of the Old Testament often associated illness and suffering with sinfulness and guilt, and felt that God was punishing them for their sins. A deeper reading of the Old Testament reveals the more trusting, hopeful faith of the Israelites in God as the source of healing. The prayer of the psalmist reflects this trust and confidence:

> Have pity on me, Lord,
>   for I am weak;
>   heal me, LORD, for my bones are
>   trembling.   **Psalm 6:3**

> The LORD sustains them on their
>   sickbed,
>   allays the malady when they
>   are ill.   **Psalm 41:4**

The Israelites, just as their contemporaries—and as all peoples of all times, past, present, and future—sought to make sense of suffering. Isaiah was one of the major prophets of Israel. He spoke of one, a suffering servant, who would come and suffer for God's people. In his suffering all would be saved:

> Because of his affliction
> he shall see the light in fullness
>   of days;
> Through his suffering, my servant
>   shall justify many,
> and their guilt he shall bear.
> Therefore I will give him his portion
>   among the great.
>   **Isaiah 53:11–12**

Illness, suffering, and death exist because of **original sin.** God does wield a magic wand to remove suffering and sickness; but he has promised that the time of pain—of suffering, illness, and death—will end. During the period of suffering, God is present with us as our source of healing, comfort, and hope.

Reflecting on the mystery of suffering, the Church teaches this same faith:

> Although closely linked with the human condition, sickness cannot as a general rule be regarded as punishment inflicted on each individual for personal sins (see John 9:3). Christ himself, who is without sin, in fulfilling the words of Isaiah took on all the wounds of his passion and shared in all human

pain (see Isaiah 53:3–5). [O]ur afflictions seem but momentary and slight when compared to the greatness of the eternal glory for which they prepare us (see 2 Corinthians 4:17).

Pastoral Care of the Sick, 2

and recovery of sight to the blind,
   to let the oppressed go free,
and to proclaim a year acceptable
   to the Lord."

Luke 4:18–19
(quoting Isaiah 61:1–2)

The New Testament

Christians believe that Jesus is the "suffering servant" promised by God through the prophet Isaiah. In the synagogue in Nazareth, Jesus announced his mission by reading from the scroll of the prophet Isaiah:

"The Spirit of the Lord is upon me,
because he has anointed me
   to bring glad tidings to the poor.
He has sent me to proclaim liberty
   to captives

...Christ as Healer and Physician...

There are many stories in the Gospels that reveal that God is present among us as our "healer" in times of our suffering. Jesus makes the blind to see, the lame to walk, the deaf to hear, and the mute to speak. He reaches out to touch and cure those suffering with fever and other illnesses. On several occasions, he compassionately frees those possessed by demons, and raises the dead back to life.

Stories of Suffering and Healing

God reveals himself as the source of healing, not the one who brings illness and suffering into our lives. Think about and write about times when you, your family members, or your friends were faced with a serious illness or another form of suffering. How were you or they comforted or helped during the illness? What effect did that experience have upon your view of suffering in the world? On your relationship with God?

All of Jesus' healings proclaim "a year acceptable to the Lord." Jesus' miracles of healing are signs of the kingdom of God among us. Through them the Spirit invites people to trust in God. All point to his suffering, death on the cross, and resurrection, the ultimate victory of the "suffering servant of God" over sin and death.

READING THE BIBLE

Select and read one of these gospel passages. Describe the healing that takes place.

Luke 7:11–17	Mark 2:5–12
Mark 5:25–43	Mark 8:22–25
John 9:6–7	Mark 1:40–41
Mark 9:17–29	

.... Discuss:

What does each passage reveal about God? How does that insight into the mystery of God affect your ability to deal with suffering?

The Church: The Instrument of God's Healing, Sharers in ...... the Sufferings of Christ ......

Jesus makes his disciples sharers in his ministry of healing. "They drove out many demons," the Gospel according to Mark tells us, "and they anointed with oil many who were sick and cured them" (Mark 6:13).

After his resurrection, the Risen Lord commissioned his disciples, saying, "Go into the whole world and proclaim the gospel to every creature" (Mark 16:15). Describing their work, Jesus concludes, "They will lay hands on the sick, and they will recover" (Mark 16:18).

From its beginning, the Church has continued this work of Jesus. The apostles and first Christians clearly remembered and fulfilled Jesus' command, "Cure the sick" (Matthew 10:8). In the Letter to James, we read:

> Is anyone among you suffering? He should pray. Is anyone in good spirits? He should sing praise. Is anyone among you sick? He should summon the presbyters of the church, and they should pray over him and anoint [him] with oil in the name of the Lord, and the prayer of faith will save the sick person, and the Lord will raise him up. If he has committed any sins, he will be forgiven.
>
> **James 5:13–15**

But this work was not their work alone. It was the work of the Lord, the work of the Spirit. In writing about the gifts the Spirit shares with the Church, Paul teaches:

Dealing with the Mystery of Suffering or Not Dealing with It

Dr. Jack Kevorkian assists people who are suffering by helping them end their lives through the use of assisted-suicide devices. Compare Kevorkian's approach to suffering with the message of Sacred Scripture.

> There are different kinds of spiritual gifts but the same Spirit. . . . To each individual the manifestation of the Spirit is given for some benefit. To one is given through the Spirit the expression of wisdom; . . . to another gifts of healing by the one Spirit.
> **1 Corinthians 12:4, 7–9**

Throughout his earthly ministry, Jesus reminded his followers that being his disciples included sharing in his suffering. They were to take up their cross and follow him. They would be blessed when they suffered for the sake of righteousness. Trusting in Jesus, they would keep hope amidst suffering. This faith and vision of suffering are reflected in the First Letter of Peter. He writes:

> Beloved, do not be surprised that a trial by fire is occurring among you, as if something strange were happening to you. But rejoice to the extent that you share in the sufferings of Christ, so that when his glory is revealed you may also rejoice exultantly.
> **1 Peter 4:12–13**

Having faith in this meaning of the mystery of sickness and suffering revealed in Sacred Scripture builds in us the virtue of **compassion.** The word *compassion* comes from the Latin words *passio* and *cum*, which mean "suffering" and "with." A compassionate person shares in the suffering of others.

It is out of this tradition of the mystery of suffering and healing, passed on by the apostles and the Church, that we have and celebrate the sacrament of the Anointing of the Sick.

The New Adam

The suffering and death of Jesus on the cross gave a new meaning to suffering and death. All suffering is now united to the suffering of Jesus Christ.

Sickness, suffering, and death came into the world through the original sin of our first parents, Adam and Eve. But Jesus, the new Adam, takes the miseries and sufferings of all people onto himself. "He took away our infirmities and bore our diseases" (Matthew 8:17).

 Discuss:

We are called by Jesus to be his disciples and to take up our cross and follow him (Matthew 10:38).

(CCC, 1514–1523)

The Sacrament of the Anointing of the Sick

Since apostolic times the Church has reached out in Christ's name to the sick and dying. The celebration of the sacrament of the **Anointing of the Sick** continues the healing ministry of Christ. The Anointing of the Sick strengthens our faith and trust in God when we are seriously ill or dying or weakened by old age. We receive the grace to face our sickness and even our dying with courage and hope. We believe that God is always with us.

Recipients and Ministers of This Sacrament

The celebration of the sacrament of the Anointing of the Sick in our life as Christians became, in the past, very limited. It was seen as the sacrament to be celebrated only at the extreme moment of our life when death was imminent. Because of this, it was called Extreme Unction.

Recipients of the Anointing of the Sick. The Anointing of the Sick is not just a sacrament for those who are at the point of death. It "is the proper sacrament for those Christians whose health is seriously impaired by sickness or old age" (*Pastoral Care of the Sick,* 97). Another appropriate time to receive this sacrament is just before a serious operation. (See CCC, 1515.) In the introduction to the *Pastoral Care of the Sick,* the bishops write:

> Those who are seriously ill need the special help of God's grace in this time of anxiety, lest they be broken

in spirit and, under the pressure of temptation, perhaps weakened in their faith.

That is why, through the sacrament of anointing, Christ strengthens the faithful who are afflicted by illness, providing them with the strongest means of support.

Pastoral Care of the Sick, 5

The faithful who are seriously ill, therefore, should seek to celebrate this sacrament at the beginning of their illness and while they are able to actively participate in its celebration. The sacrament of anointing may be repeated:

a. when the sick person recovers after being anointed and, at a later time, becomes sick again;

b. when during the same illness the condition of the sick person becomes more serious.

In the case of a person who is chronically ill, or elderly and in a weakened condition, the sacrament of anointing may be repeated when in the pastoral judgment of the priest the condition of the sick person warrants the repetition of the sacrament.

Pastoral Care of the Sick, 102

If the sacrament of anointing is not celebrated during the course of a serious illness, " 'as soon as anyone of the faithful begins to be in danger of death from sickness or old age, the fitting time for him to receive this sacrament has certainly already arrived' " (*Constitution on the Sacred Liturgy,* 73).

Ministers of the Anointing of the Sick. Priests (bishops and presbyters) are ministers of the Anointing of the Sick. The sick are encouraged to call the priest when necessary. Wherever the sacrament is celebrated—in a hospital, in the family home, or in the church— friends and family are encouraged to be prayerfully present at the time of anointing as a source of support. (See CCC, 1517.)

The Celebration of the Anointing of the Sick

The sacrament of the Anointing of the Sick, like all the other sacraments, is a liturgical and communal celebration. It is most appropriately celebrated within the Eucharist whenever possible.

••••••• Liturgy of the Word •••••••
The Liturgy of the Word is preceded by an act of repentance, which opens the celebration. The Spirit of God awakens the faith of the sick person and of the community.

••••••• Liturgy of Anointing •••••••
The Liturgy of the Word is followed by the Liturgy of Anointing. It always includes these elements: the priest lays his hands on the sick, prays over them in the faith of the Church (this is the epiclesis prayer proper to this sacrament) and anoints the sick with oil blessed, if possible, by the bishop. (See CCC, 1519.)

Prayer of Faith. The community makes its prayer of faith in response to God's word and in a spirit of trust (see James 5:14–15). "In the rites for the sick, it is the people of God who pray in faith. The entire Church is made present in this community—represented by at least the priest, family, and others— assembled to pray for those to be anointed" (*Pastoral Care of the Sick,* 105).

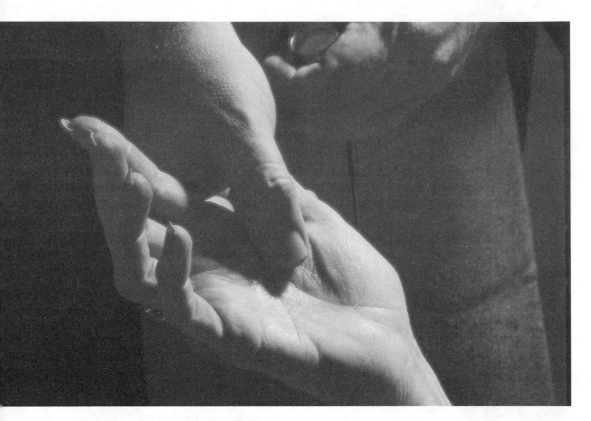

Laying On of Hands. "With this gesture the priest indicates that this particular person is the object of the Church's prayer of faith. The laying on of hands is clearly a sign of blessing, as we pray that by the power of God's healing grace the sick person may be restored to health or at least strengthened in time of illness. The laying on of hands is also an invocation: the Church prays for the coming of the Holy Spirit upon the sick person" (*Pastoral Care of the Sick,* 106).

Anointing with Oil. The forehead of the sick person's head is anointed by the priest, who says:

> Through this holy anointing may the Lord in his love and mercy help you with the grace of the Holy Spirit.

The priest continues with the anointing of the sick person's hands, saying:

> May the Lord who frees you from sin save you and raise you up.

The Effects of the Sacrament

Healing is one of the gifts of the Holy Spirit. Through this sacrament the Holy Spirit is called upon to heal our body and soul. We receive forgiveness of our sin, if we are "not able to obtain it through the sacrament of Penance" and "the restoration of health, if it is conducive to the salvation of [our] soul" (CCC, 1532).

The Holy Spirit invites us to renew our trust and faith in God, and strengthens us to face the temptations arising from our suffering or approaching death. We are united to the passion and suffering of Jesus Christ. Our suffering becomes a participation in the "saving" work of Jesus.

When the Church celebrates the sacrament with us, we are joined with the communion of saints and all the faithful who pray for us. We contribute to the good of the People of God—the sanctification of the Church and the good of all people in the Church by offering our suffering through Christ to God.

Viaticum

The Anointing of the Sick is also celebrated with those who are very near to death. For this reason, it is also called the *sacramentum exeuntium,* or the "sacrament of those departing." The Church offers the Eucharist as viaticum to the person about to leave this life. This is the Body and Blood of the Lord "to take with them" as food for their final journey. (The word *viaticum* means "food for the journey.") "The sacrament of Christ once dead and now risen, the Eucharist is here the sacrament of passing over from death to life, from this world to the Father (see John 13:1)" (CCC, 1524).

The Sacraments of Initiation (Baptism, Confirmation, and the Eucharist) make us sharers in the life of Christ. The Sacraments of Healing (Penance and the Anointing of the Sick) and the Eucharist as viaticum prepare "for our heavenly homeland." They are the sacraments that complete the earthly pilgrimage.

> This saying is trustworthy:
> If we have died with him
>   we shall also live with him;
> if we persevere
>   we shall also reign with him.
> **2 Timothy 2:11–12**

What the Documents Say

In reflecting on human sickness and its meaning in the mystery of salvation, the Church teaches:

Suffering and illness have always been among the greatest problems that trouble the human spirit. Christians feel and experience pain as do all other people; yet their faith helps them to grasp more deeply the mystery of suffering and to bear their pain with greater courage.

Pastoral Care of the Sick,
General Introduction, 1

Discuss:

In what ways does your Christian faith help you deal with your own pain? In what ways does it help you help others deal with their pain?

Prayer

❖ ❖ ❖

Prayerfully read this prayer of blessing that the priest or bishop says for the blessing of the oil of the sick. It professes the faith of Christians in the presence of God in our midst as the source of healing and strength as we face sickness and suffering.

God of all consolation,
you chose and sent your Son
    to heal the world.
Graciously listen to our prayer
    of faith:
send the power of your Holy Spirit,
    the Consoler,
into this precious oil, this soothing
    ointment,
this rich gift, this fruit of the earth.

Bless this oil and sanctify it
    for our use.

Make this oil a remedy for all who
    are anointed with it;
heal them in body, in soul, and
    in spirit,
and deliver them from every
    affliction.
We ask this through our Lord Jesus
    Christ, your Son,
who lives and reigns with you
    and the Holy Spirit,
one God for ever and ever. Amen.

ROMAN MISSAL

IMPORTANT TERMS TO KNOW

Anointing of the Sick—the Sacrament of Healing that strengthens our faith and trust in God when we are seriously ill, dying, or weakened by old age; unites us to the passion of Christ; forgives our sins if we are not able to celebrate Penance; and prepares us for our passing over to eternal life

compassion—virtue of sharing in the sufferings of others, witnessing to God's healing presence with them

original sin—the first sin by which Adam lost his state of original holiness and justice he received from God, not only for himself but for all human beings; the state or condition of sin into which all people are born since the time of Adam's turning away from God

sacramentum exeuntium—Latin for "sacrament of those departing"

CHAPTER SUMMARY

The sacrament of the Anointing of the Sick is one of the two Sacraments of Healing of the Church. In this chapter we learned:

1. Healing is associated with forgiveness and God's mercy and love.

2. The mission and ministry of Jesus involved healing. He gave the authority and power to heal to his disciples. Healing is a gift of the Holy Spirit.

3. The Anointing of the Sick is given not only to those at the point of death but also to the sick and to those frail with old age, or in preparation for surgery. It can be received more than once during an illness.

4. The sacrament can be celebrated at home, in a hospital, or at church. The family and friends are encouraged to be present and support the sick person with prayers.

5. Only priests (bishops and presbyters) are ministers of the Anointing of the Sick.

6. The principal elements of the rite are the laying of hands on the sick by the priest, praying over the sick by the priest in the faith of the Church, and the anointing of the forehead and hands with the blessed oil.

7. The effects of the sacrament are healing and strengthening of the body and soul as a gift of the Holy Spirit, being united to the sufferings of Christ, contributing to the good of the Church by the prayers and sufferings offered up to God through Christ, and through the intercessions of the communion of saints, preparing for our final journey home to God.

EXPLORING OUR CATHOLIC FAITH

1. Listening to God's Word

1 Peter 4:13 says, "But rejoice to the extent that you share in the sufferings of Christ, so that when his glory is revealed you may also rejoice exultantly." It seems contradictory to say that suffering is good. Discuss how sharing in Christ's suffering makes you worthy to share in his glory.

2. Understanding the Teachings of the Catholic Church

In the General Introduction to the rites of *Pastoral Care of the Sick,* the Church teaches that "Christians feel and experience pain as do all other people; yet their faith helps them to grasp more deeply the mystery of suffering and to bear their pain with greater courage" (*Pastoral Care of the Sick,* 1). What does the sacrament of the Anointing of the Sick help us understand about the mystery of suffering?

3. Reflecting on Our Catholic Faith

Many people have experienced pain and suffering in their lives. Reflect on your own experiences of pain and suffering. How did your Christian faith help you face that pain and suffering? How will it help you face pain and suffering in the future? Write your reflections in your journal.

4. Living Our Catholic Faith

How can your faith help you show compassion to a close friend or family member who is sick or suffering?

CHAPTER 9

Holy Orders

I remind you to stir into flame the gift of God
that you have through the imposition of my hands.

2 Timothy 1:6

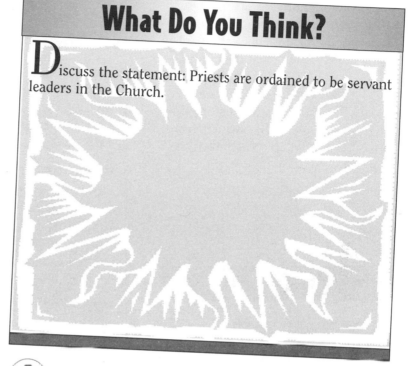

Discuss the statement: Priests are ordained to be servant leaders in the Church.

One of the great leaders of the Catholic Church in the United States was Cardinal Joseph L. Bernardin (1928–1996). Upon his death, Pope John Paul II wrote:

> I am confident that the example of the Cardinal's devoted service as priest in his native Charleston, as Archbishop of Cincinnati and Archbishop of Chicago, his untiring work as General Secretary and President of the Bishop's Conference, his generous cooperation with the holy see, as well as his witness of dignity and hope in the face of the mystery of suffering and death will inspire all who knew him to ever greater fidelity to Christ and to the gospel of our redemption.

In what ways do you serve others? What is the most important thing you have done for someone else? Why do you value it as the "most important"?

KEY TERMS

college of bishops

consecrate

Holy Orders

order

ordination

presbyter

presbyterium

Sacraments at the Service of Communion

Cardinal Joseph L. Bernardin. He was born in 1928, ordained to the priesthood in 1952, and ordained a bishop in 1966. He was named Archbishop of Cincinnati in 1972 and Archbishop of Chicago in 1982. He became a cardinal in 1983.

Cardinal Bernardin has been recognized and honored as one of the great contemporary servant leaders of the Catholic Church. Pope John Paul II said, "I am confident that the example of the Cardinal's devoted service as a priest . . . will inspire all who knew him." In this chapter we will study the sacrament of Holy Orders, which is one of the Church's two Sacraments at the Service of Communion.

(Catechism of the Catholic Church, 1533–1535)

Sacraments at the Service of Communion

The Sacraments of Initiation—Baptism, Confirmation, and the Eucharist—call, anoint, and nourish all the faithful to live a life in Christ, who is priest, prophet, and king. The person fully initiated by these sacraments shares in the life of Christ, becomes his disciple, receives a vocation to holiness, and is sent on the mission of evangelizing the world.

Holy Orders and Matrimony, the two **Sacraments at the Service of Communion, consecrate** some of the faithful to live their Christian initiation by serving the whole Body of Christ. The word *consecrate* comes from two Latin words meaning "to set aside for a holy purpose." Holy Orders consecrates a man "to feed the Church by the word and grace of God." Christian spouses are consecrated "for the duties and dignity of their state" through marriage.

(CCC, 1539–1553)

The Priesthood in Sacred Scripture

Sacred Scripture reveals God's chosen people to be a kingdom of priests. In the establishment of the Covenant at Mount Sinai the Lord says to Moses:

> "Therefore, if you hearken to my voice and keep my covenant, you shall be my special possession, dearer to me than all other people, though all the earth is mine. You shall be to me a kingdom of priests, a holy nation." **Exodus 19:5–6**

God's plan is fulfilled in Jesus Christ, who is the "one mediator between God and the human race" (1 Timothy 2:5).

In Christ the new and perfect covenant has been ratified. He has called and established a new People of God who are " 'a chosen race, a royal priesthood, a holy nation, a people of his own' " (1 Peter 2:9).

Priesthood in the Old Covenant

The tradition of the priesthood serving the People of God is rooted in the Old Covenant, in the person and work of Melchizedek; the tribe of Levi, or the Levites; and the seventy elders (Numbers 11:24–25). Priests of the Old Covenant:

❏ led liturgical service,
❏ offered gifts and sacrifices for sins,
❏ proclaimed the Word of God, and
❏ restored communication with God by sacrifices and prayers.

Melchizedek. Melchizedek is first mentioned in Genesis 14:18–20. As the king and high priest of Salem, which is later to be known as Jerusalem, he brings out gifts of bread and wine as an offering to Abraham. He says a special prayer of blessing for Abraham.

For Christians and Jews alike Melchizedek is a "priest of God Most High." The Christian tradition considers Melchizedek as a prefiguration of the priesthood of Christ, the unique " 'high priest after the order of Melchizedek' (Hebrews 5:10)" (CCC, 1544).

Levites. God tells Moses to set apart the Levites (Numbers 1:48–53) and place them in charge of the Dwelling of the commandments. In Joshua 13:33, the tribe of Levi is given the special privilege of receiving God as their heritage.

Malachi, reminding God's people of the true role and ministry of the priesthood, describes how the priests of his time have fallen short of their responsibilities:

> And now, O priests, this
>   commandment is for you: . . .
> I have a covenant with Levi,
>   says the LORD of hosts. . . .
> But you have turned aside from the
>   way,
>   and have caused many to falter by
>   your instruction;
> You have made void the covenant of
>   Levi,
>   says the LORD of hosts.
>   **Malachi 2:1, 4, 8**

Priesthood of Jesus Christ

"Everything that the priesthood of the Old Covenant prefigured finds its fulfillment in Christ Jesus" (CCC, 1544).

The sacrifice of Jesus as priest and victim was offered once and for all.

> He has no need, as did the high priests, to offer sacrifice day after day, first for his own sins and then for those of the people; he did that once for all when he offered himself.
>
> **Hebrews 7:27**

Jesus, because he remains forever, has a priesthood which does not pass away. Therefore he is always able to save those who approach God through him, since he forever lives to make intercession for them.

Through the ministerial priesthood Christ builds up and leads the Church. He himself is "present to his Church as Head of his Body, Shepherd of his flock, high priest of the redemptive sacrifice, Teacher of Truth" (CCC, 1548).

Priesthood in the Church

Ministerial Priesthood. The priest "acts in the name and person of Christ the Head" (CCC, 1591). The one priesthood of

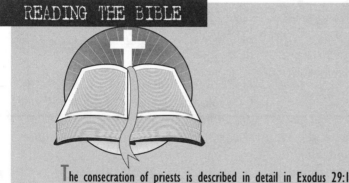

READING THE BIBLE

The consecration of priests is described in detail in Exodus 29:1–43 and Leviticus 8:1–36. Choose one of the passages and write a summary of what took place. Explain the role of animals, clothing, and anointing.

.... Discuss:
Compare these passages with Hebrews 9:1–28, and explain how Jesus is the priest and victim of the sacrifice.

The bishops gathered at the Second Vatican Council taught this about the common priesthood of the faithful and the ministerial priesthood:

> Though they differ essentially and not only in degree, the common priesthood of the faithful and the ministerial or hierarchical priesthood are none the less ordered to one another; each in its own proper way shares in the one priesthood of Christ. The ministerial priest, by the sacred power that he has, forms and rules the priestly people; in the person of Christ he effects the eucharistic sacrifice and offers it to God in the name of all the people. The faithful indeed, by virtue of their royal priesthood, participate in the offering of the Eucharist. They exercise that priesthood, too, by the reception of the sacraments, prayer, and thanksgiving, the witness of a holy life, abnegation and active charity.
>
> *Constitution on the Church,* 10

Discuss:

Think about what you did today. Relate those activities to your "priestly" identity.

Christ is made present through the ministerial priesthood. "Only Christ is the true priest," teaches Saint Thomas Aquinas, "the others being only his ministers" (*On Hebrews,* 8, 4).

The ministerial priesthood represents Christ and the Church. The ordained minister is a minister not only of Christ but of the whole Church.

The priest also acts in the name of the whole Church. At liturgy, the priest both represents Christ before the assembly of the faithful and acts in the name of the whole Church. He presents the prayer of the Church to God. This does not mean the priest is simply the delegate of the faithful. "It is because the ministerial priesthood represents Christ that it can represent the Church" (CCC, 1553). It is the Body of Christ, Head and members, that "prays and offers herself" (CCC, 1553).

Priesthood of All the Faithful.
Through Baptism all the faithful share in the common priesthood of Christ and the Church. All the faithful are consecrated to be "built into a spiritual house to be a holy priesthood to offer spiritual sacrifices acceptable to God through Jesus Christ" (1 Peter 2:5).

"Christ is the source of all priesthood: the priest of the old law was a figure of Christ," Saint Thomas Aquinas wrote, "and the priest of the new law acts in the person of Christ" (*Summa Theologica,* III, 22, 4c).

Both the priesthood of all the faithful and the ministerial priesthood serve God in their own particular way. But the difference is that the ministerial priesthood is set up to serve the common priesthood of believers.

The Sacrament of Holy Orders

Jesus chose the Twelve to lead his followers under the leadership of Peter. He sent them out together to preach, teach, and baptize as co-workers. Jesus gave the Church the sacrament of Holy Orders to continue that work in his name.

Holy Orders

The sacrament of **Holy Orders** "is the sacrament through which the mission entrusted by Christ to his apostles continues to be exercised in the Church until the end of time: thus it is the sacrament of apostolic ministry" (CCC, 1536).

There are three degrees of Holy Orders: episcopate, or **order** of bishop; presbyterate, or order of priest; and diaconate, or order of deacon.

The word ordo (in English, *order*) is a word used in Roman antiquity that designated an established civil, or governing, body. **Ordination,** or ordinatio, refers to the incorporation into an order. The Church adopted these words and concepts and applied them to those chosen to be the servant leaders of the church community.

We use the word *ordination* to refer strictly to the consecration of those men who are incorporated into the orders of bishop, priest, or deacon through the sacrament of Holy Orders. The laying on of hands by the bishop and the consecratory prayer make up the visible sign of this ordination. This sacramental ordination sets the ordained minister aside to serve the whole church community. It confers a gift of the Holy Spirit that permits the exercise of "sacred power" that comes only from Christ himself for his Church.

Episcopate— Fullness of the ..... Sacrament of Holy Orders .....

Bishops receive the fullness of the sacrament of Holy Orders. Episcopal consecration confers not only the office of sanctifying but also the office of teaching and ruling.

Bishops are successors of the apostles and are members of the **college of bishops.** They are the true and authentic teachers of the faith. They "share in the apostolic responsibility and mission of the whole Church under the authority of the Pope, successor of St. Peter" (CCC, 1594). Appointed by the pope, the bishop of Rome, a bishop is the visible head of a local, or particular, church community that is entrusted to him.

Presbyterate— ..... Co-workers of the Bishop .....

Priests are appointed by their bishop to assist him in his apostolic mission and responsibilities. Priests are co-workers with their bishop. They represent their bishop and take on their duties in their particular locale or ecclesial office entrusted to them by the bishop. Together they form a sacerdotal college, or **presbyterium.**

Through the sacrament of Holy Orders priests are consecrated to preach the Gospel, shepherd the faithful, and celebrate divine worship. They are anointed with the Holy Spirit and signed with a special character and " 'configured to Christ the priest in such a way that they are able to act in the person of Christ the head' (*Decree on Ministry and Life of Priests,* 2)" (CCC, 1563).

Diaconate—
.... The Order of Service ....

Deacons do not receive the ministerial priesthood. They assist in the celebration of the Eucharist by proclaiming the Gospel, preaching, and distributing Holy Communion. They baptize, and bless and assist at marriages. They preside over funerals. Most importantly, they assist their bishop with the works of service of the Church.

Since the Second Vatican Council, the Latin Church has restored the permanent diaconate, which the Church in the East had always maintained. The permanent diaconate is conferred on married or single men who do not aspire to become priests or bishops. If single, they are to remain celibate.

The Celebration of the Sacrament

The sacrament of Holy Orders is celebrated by the laying on of hands and the praying of a special prayer of consecration by the bishop.

Other rites are also celebrated:

❏ The priest and bishop are anointed with chrism.
❏ The bishop receives the Book of the Gospels, the ring, the miter, and the crosier, or pastoral staff. This is a sign of his apostolic mission to proclaim the Word of God, his fidelity to the Church, and his office as shepherd of the Lord's flock.

❏ The hands of the priest are anointed with oil. He is also presented with the paten and chalice, symbolic of the people's offering, which he is called to present to God.
❏ The deacon is given the Book of the Gospels for his mission to proclaim the Gospel of Christ.

Because of the importance of Holy Orders to the life of the Church, this sacrament should be celebrated on a Sunday, in the cathedral, within the Eucharist. As many of the faithful as possible should be invited to take part.

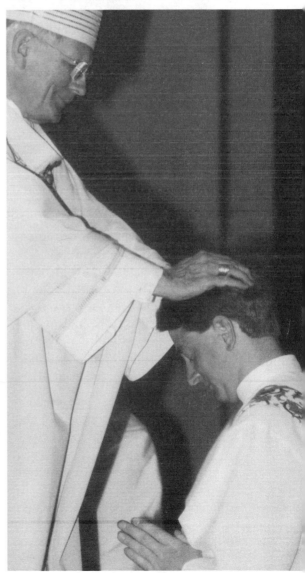

...The Minister of the Sacrament...

Only validly ordained bishops who are in the line of apostolic succession validly confer the three degrees of the sacrament of Holy Orders. The bishop, as successor of the apostles, hands on the "gift of the Spirit" and the "apostolic line," in keeping with the way Christ chose the apostles to continue his work in the world.

...The Recipient of the Sacrament...

No one has a right to the sacrament of Holy Orders. Candidates are called by God to this ministry. And the Church's authority alone has the responsibility and right to call someone to receive orders.

"Only a baptized man *(vir)* validly receives sacred ordination" (Code of Canon Law, canon 1024). Because Jesus chose men to be his apostles and they in turn only chose men to be their successors, the ordination of women is not possible.

The Rites of the Sacrament

Ordination of Bishops. In the ordination of a bishop, the consecrating bishops lay their hands on the bishop-elect in silence. Then a opened Book of the Gospels is held over the bishop-elect as the principal consecrating bishop, with hands extended, prays the prayer of consecration. These essential words of the prayer are said by all the consecrating bishops:

> So now pour out upon this chosen one
> that power which is from you,
> the governing Spirit
> whom you gave to your beloved Son,
>   Jesus Christ,
> who founded the Church in every place
>   to be your temple,
> for the unceasing glory and praise of
>   your name.   *Ordination of a Bishop*

The imposition of hands and the words of consecration give the bishop the grace of the Holy Spirit and a special character that makes him a visible presence of Christ as teacher, shepherd, and priest.

The head of the newly ordained bishop is then anointed with chrism and he is given the Book of the Gospels. Next he is given three symbols of his office: the ring, the mitre, and the pastoral staff. Finally, he is invited to take his place at the bishop's chair, the symbol of his leadership.

Ordination of Priests. The ordaining bishop lays his hands on each candidate in silence. If there are other priests present, they lay hands on the candidates after the bishop. This shows that they belong to the order of **presbyters** and share in the priesthood of Jesus Christ. The ordaining bishop then prays the prayer of consecration. These are the essential words of the prayer:

> Almighty Father,
> grant to this servant of yours
> the dignity of priesthood.
> Renew within him the Spirit of
>   holiness.
> As a co-worker with the order of
>   bishops
> may he be faithful to the ministry
> that he receives from you, Lord God,
> and be to others a model of right
>   conduct.   *Ordination of a Priest*

The bishop then vests the newly ordained priest with stole and chasuble, which are symbols of the priest's sacred duties of preaching the Gospel and leading the People of God in offering sacrifice to God. Next the palms of the hands of the newly ordained priest are anointed with chrism.

The promise of obedience made to the bishop at the moment of ordination and the kiss of peace from the bishop at the end of the ordination liturgy give witness that the bishop considers the newly ordained priests his co-workers.

Ordination of Deacons. In the ordination of deacons, the candidates kneel before the ordaining bishop, who lays his hands on their heads in silence. He then prays the consecratory prayer. These are the essential words of the prayer:

> Lord,
> send forth upon them the Holy Spirit,
> that they may be strengthened
> by the gift of your sevenfold grace
> to carry out faithfully the work of
>   the ministry.   *Ordination of a Deacon*

An assisting priest or deacon then vests the newly ordained deacon with the deacon's stole and dalmatic. The vested deacon then kneels before the bishop, who places the Book of the Gospels in the newly ordained deacon's hands, saying:

> Receive the Gospel of Christ,
> whose herald you now are.
> Believe what you read,
> teach what you believe,
> and practice what you teach.
>   *Ordination of a Deacon*

The newly ordained deacon then stands and receives the kiss of peace from the bishops and the other deacons who are present.

The Effects of the Sacrament

Indelible Character. The sacrament of Holy Orders confers an indelible character that marks the bishop, priest, and deacon. By a special grace of the Holy Spirit, this sacrament configures the ordained minister to Christ that he might "serve as Christ's instrument for his Church" (CCC, 1581).

Grace of the Holy Spirit. A second effect is the special grace of the Holy Spirit. For the bishop it is "the grace to guide and defend his Church with strength and prudence as a father and pastor, with gratuitous love for all and a preferential love for the poor, the sick, and the needy" (CCC, 1586). For the priest, it is the grace to act as co-workers with the bishops to celebrate the sacraments and assist the bishop as a servant of the Church. For the deacon, it is the grace of dedication to God's people, and to the bishop and priests through the service of assisting at the liturgy, proclaiming the Gospel, and performing works of charity.

Prayer

❖ ❖ ❖

The following is part of the prayer of consecration prayer at the ordination of a bishop. Pray it for your bishop, that he may be blessed with the grace to serve the Church.

Father, you know all hearts.
You have chosen your servant
for the office of bishop.
May he be a shepherd to your flock,
and a high priest blameless in your sight,
ministering to you night and day;
may he always gain
the blessing of your favor
and offer the gifts of your holy Church.
Amen.

REVIEW

IMPORTANT TERMS TO KNOW

college of bishops—the episcopal college; the unity of the bishops together with the pope; it is the expression of the variety and universality of the People of God, and of the unity of the Body of Christ.

consecrate—to set aside for a holy, or sacred, purpose

Holy Orders—the Sacrament at the Service of Communion that incorporates a man into the order of bishop, priest, or deacon

order—the English word for the word *ordo,* used in Roman antiquity to designate an established civil, or governing, body; in the Church the word refers to the three orders of bishop, priest, and deacon

ordination—the word used for the incorporation into an order; in the Church this refers to those incorporated into a particular order through ordination by a bishop

presbyter—a member of the order of priests, co-workers with the bishop.

presbyterium—the college of priests under the leadership of the bishop; together they exercise responsibility for the local, or particular, church community entrusted to the bishop.

Sacraments at the Service of Communion—Holy Orders and Matrimony; the two sacraments of the Church that consecrate some of the faithful to live their Christian initiation by serving the whole Body of Christ

CHAPTER SUMMARY

The sacrament of Holy Orders is one of the Church's two Sacraments at the Service of Communion. In this chapter we learned:

1. The Sacraments at the Service of Communion are Holy Orders and Matrimony. They consecrate some of the faithful to serve the whole Body of Christ, the Church.

2. Through the sacrament of Holy Orders the mission entrusted by Christ to his apostles continues to be exercised until the end of time. The sacrament is conferred by the laying on of hands and a prayer of consecration.

3. Holy Orders consists of three degrees: episcopate, presbyterate, and diaconate.

4. Only a baptized man with the intention to live a celibate life can validly receive Holy Orders. Only a validly ordained bishop can confer the sacrament of Holy Orders in all three degrees.

5. The common priesthood of all the faithful and the ministerial priesthood are essentially different.

6. Bishops receive the fullness of the sacrament of Holy Orders. They are members of the college of bishops and head of a particular church entrusted to them.

7. Priests serve as co-workers with the bishop. They form with the bishop the presbyterium, which bears responsibility for the particular church entrusted to the bishop.

8. Deacons are not ordained to the ministerial priesthood. They are ordained to a ministry of service under the pastoral authority of the bishop.

9. The effects of Holy Orders are an indelible character that configures the ordained to Christ, and the grace of the Holy Spirit that is received according to each particular order and that strengthens the ordained for their service to the Church.

EXPLORING OUR CATHOLIC FAITH

1. Listening to God's Word

Read and reflect on Mark 10:43–45. What does this passage teach about leadership within the Church?

2. Understanding the Teachings of the Catholic Church

Read the prayers of consecration from the rites of ordination of bishops, priests, and deacons on pages 112–113 of this workbook. What do they teach about the identity and ministry of the servant leaders of our Church?

3. Reflecting on Our Catholic Faith

All the faithful share in the one priesthood of Christ. We speak of the common priesthood of all the faithful and the ministerial priesthood. What does it mean for you that you share in the priesthood of Jesus? Write your thoughts in your journal.

4. Living Our Catholic Faith

Brainstorm ways you can cooperate with priests and deacons. How does working with them reveal who we are as the Body of Christ in the world?

CHAPTER 10

Matrimony

[T]he two of them become one body.
GENESIS 2:24

Name several popular TV sitcoms that portray marriage and family life. Compare each view of marriage and family life that is portrayed with your own view.

The film *A Man for All Seasons* is based on the life of Thomas More, lord chancellor for King Henry VIII. Henry was engaged in a bitter battle with the Roman Catholic Church over his desire to divorce Catherine of Aragon. Because More placed his fidelity to God and the Church before his allegiance to Henry, he refused to support the king—at eventual cost of his life. In a scene from the film, Alice, More's wife, wants to know why he is resigning. His love for her results in silence. Alice fears that he does not trust her. But his silence, he explains, is not about trust, but love.

KEY TERMS

annulment

divorce

domestic church

fidelity

indissolubility

Matrimony

Explain why you agree or disagree that fidelity and love are at the heart of the marriage covenant?

A scene from *A Man for All Seasons,*
(Copyright © 1966 Columbia Pictures Corporation).

homas More—husband, father, lord chancellor of England—was above all else in all these roles faithful to God. Thomas's fidelity to God, to the Church, to his country, and to his family was unbreakable. On July 6, 1535, he was beheaded. He was canonized a saint of the Church in 1935 and is recognized as an inspiration and model for all Christians. In this chapter we will focus on Matrimony, the second of the Church's two Sacraments at the Service of Communion.

Marriage in God's Plan

A television commercial shows a young man and woman in an elevator. They look at each other in a flirtatious kind of way. Suddenly the commercial shows the thoughts of the couple as they think about the stages of courtship, romance, marriage, crying babies, and old age. At the realization of what is involved with marriage and commitment, the couple

Getting Ready for Marriage

The importance of Matrimony is taught by the Church in many ways. One way is the Church's insistence that those seeking to commit themselves to the married life prepare themselves adequately. At the Second Vatican Council the Church taught:

It is imperative to give suitable and timely instruction to young people, above all in the heart of their own families, about the dignity of married love, its role and its exercise, so that, having learned the value of chastity, they will be able at a suitable age to engage in honorable courtship and enter upon a marriage of their own.   *Church in the Modern World,* 49 § 3

.... Discuss:
What do the following words mean for two people preparing for marriage? What do they mean to you?

Faithfulness	**Interests**	**Intimacy**
Compromise	**Understanding**	**Sacrifice**
Spirituality	**Forgiveness**	
Children	**Career goals**	

leave the elevator in a state of total relief that their experience stopped with a simple look.

Marriage involves a major commitment. Together a man and woman join in a lifetime partnership to support one another, to be open to children, and to serve others in their capacity as husband and wife.

Marriage in the Old Testament

Marriage is a symbol and image of God, who is love (1 John 4:8) and of our relationship with God. God created us out of love and calls us to love. This is the fundamental and innate vocation of every human being.

. . Marriage in God's Plan of Creation . .

Sacred Scripture opens with the story of the creation of man and woman, who are made in the image and likeness of God (Genesis 1:26–27). This story reveals that God himself is the author of marriage.

The LORD God said: "It is not good for the man to be alone. I will make a suitable partner for him." . . .
So the LORD God cast a deep sleep on the man, and while he was asleep, he took out one of his ribs and closed up its place with flesh. The LORD God then built up into a woman the rib that he had taken from the man. When he brought her to the man, the man said:
"This one, at last, is bone of my bones
   and flesh of my flesh;
This one shall be called 'woman,'
   for out of 'her man' this one has
      been taken."
That is why a man leaves his father and mother and clings to his wife, and the two of them become one body.   **Genesis 2:18, 21–24**

Marriage is a sign of the faithful and unbreakable covenant of love of God for people. It is a covenant by which a man and a woman form an intimate communion of life and love with each other. From the very beginning a man and a woman were created to share their love for each other in familial love.

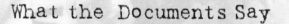

What the Documents Say

"The matrimonial covenant, by which a man and a woman establish between themselves a partnership of the whole of life, is by its nature ordered toward the good of the spouses and the procreation and education of offspring; this covenant between baptized persons has been raised by Christ the Lord to the dignity of a sacrament."

Church in the Modern World, 48

. . . . Discuss:

What does it mean to say that marriage is "a sign of the faithful and unbreakable covenant of love of God for people"?

.... Marriage under Sin ....

God's plan of creation was, in a true sense, undone by the choice of our first parents to sin. Every dimension of human life—indeed, all of creation—is affected by sin. The relationship of love and fidelity uniting spouses is not excluded.

The original sin of Adam and Eve disrupted the first marriage. The results of this sin led to the burden of pain of childbirth and the toil of work. As a result of this sin, man and woman have even a greater need to call and depend upon the grace that God never refuses anyone.

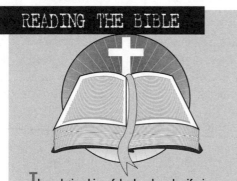

READING THE BIBLE

The relationship of husband and wife is used in the Old Testament to help us understand the mystery of God's relationship with the Israelites, his chosen people. Read Hosea 1–3; Isaiah 54 and 62; Jeremiah 2–3, and 31; Ezekiel 16 and 23; and Malachi 2:13–17.

What do these passages have to say about marriage? What do they reveal to us about our relationship with God?

Marriage in the New Testament

Just as the Old Testament used the marriage relationship to portray the relationship between God and Israel, the New Testament uses the relationship between husband and wife to help us understand the mystery of the relationship of Christ with "all mankind saved by him" (CCC, 1612).

Several stories in the Gospels help us understand Christian marriage and the mystery of God's love that it images.

...... Wedding Feast at Cana ......

In the Gospel of John the first sign Jesus performs is the miracle at the wedding of Cana (John 2:1–11). The Church looks upon this story as confirming that marriage is good and is a sign of the presence of Christ.

.... Marriage and Divorce ....

Some Pharisees questioned Jesus, asking whether according to the Law a man could divorce his wife for any cause whatever. Their intent was to embarrass Jesus and pit him against an accepted practice of his day. Jesus replied by clearly teaching the purpose of marriage in God's plan of creation, saying, "Therefore, what God has joined together, no human being must separate. . . . I say to you, whoever divorces his wife (unless the marriage is unlawful) and marries another commits adultery" (Matthew 19:6, 9).

.... Christ and the Church ....

Paul compares the relationship of Christian spouses to Christ's relationship with the Church. In writing to the Christian community in Ephesus, he sums up his teaching on marriage:

This is a great mystery, but I speak in reference to Christ and the church. In any case, each one of you should love his wife as himself, and the wife should respect her husband.

Ephesians 5:32–33

The entire Christian life reveals the spousal relationship between Christ and the Church. (See CCC, 1617.) Through Baptism we enter into a relationship with Christ and the Church. At the Eucharist we share in the wedding feast, sharing the bread and wine of eternal life. Matrimony is the living sign of the covenant of Christ and the Church.

Virginity

Some of the faithful are called by God to live a life of virginity. The Gospel of Matthew records an invitation by Jesus to live such a life "for the sake of the kingdom of heaven" (Matthew 19:12). The person who lives a chaste and celibate life is a powerful sign of the kingdom to come. Their lives are visible reminders of the passing away of this world and the permanency of the life to come.

(CCC, 1621–1658)

The Sacrament of Matrimony

Christ raised marriage to the dignity of a sacrament. The sacrament of **Matrimony** calls and consecrates a Christian man and woman to serve the whole Church as a living sign of the unity and love between Christ and the Church. The love of God for his people is most fully revealed in Christ's Paschal mystery. Christian spouses are called and consecrated to give witness to that love by living as signs of Christ's love within the Church.

The Ministers of the Sacrament

The sacrament of Matrimony is a unique sacrament because the ministers of the sacrament are the spouses themselves who express their consent before the Church. In the Eastern liturgy the priest or bishop "crowns" the bride and groom after they express their consent to each other. The epiclesis prayer asks God's grace and blessing on the new couple, especially the bride. The Holy Spirit is invoked to seal their covenant and to express their communion of love in Christ and the Church.

Rite of Marriage

The celebration of marriage normally takes place during the Eucharist. As Christ is united to the Church, his bride, couples seal their consent and unity with the unity of Christ and the Church in the Eucharist.

...... Matrimonial Consent ......

The Rite of Marriage begins with the priest or deacon asking the couple:

Have you come here freely and without reservation to give yourselves to each other in marriage?

Will you love and honor each other as man and wife for the rest of your life?

Will you accept children lovingly from God, and bring them up according to the law of Christ and his Church? *Rite of Marriage*

All the questions focus on what a true Christian marriage is all about. The spouses are to freely and knowingly enter into their marriage covenant. If this free consent is lacking, there is no marriage.

The consent between the bride and groom is usually expressed through promises. Joining hands the bride and bridegroom individually promise each other:

I, (name), take you (name), to be my (wife) husband. I promise to be true to you in good times and in bad, in sickness and in health. I will love you and honor you all the days of my life. *Rite of Marriage*

The celebration of the Rite of Marriage is a liturgical act. It takes place before a witness authorized by the Church (usually a priest or deacon), the witnesses, and the community of the faithful. It creates rights and duties in the Church that govern the relationship between the spouses, and between the spouses and their children.

The Effects of Matrimony

The spouses receive the grace to live their marriage covenant. The married couple have been chosen and consecrated by the Spirit to be public witnesses to God's faithful love for people and Christ's faithful love for his Church. The married couple have their own special gifts in the Church.

Unity and Indissolubility. The marriage bond or consent is sealed by God. It is **indissoluble.** A marriage that is concluded and consummated between baptized persons is irrevocable and can never be dissolved. The grace received through this sacrament strengthens the love and unity of a marriage. It helps each spouse attain holiness in their married and family life.

Polygamy is also incompatible with the unity of marriage. Polygamy is having more than one marriage partner.

It contradicts God's law that a marriage is a unique and exclusive love union between one man and one woman.

Because the sacrament of Marriage is indissoluble, the remarriage of persons divorced from a living, lawful spouse is against God's law and the law of the Church. Such spouses who remarry without an **annulment** from the Church are not separated from the Church but they cannot receive eucharistic communion. If such persons do not remarry without an annulment, they remain part of the life of the Church and can participate in the sacramental life of the Church. The couple can celebrate the sacrament of Penance if they choose to repent and return to a state of complete celibate living.

Fidelity. Christian marriage is a sign of Christ's unconditional faithful love for his Body, the Church. The love of the couple is to foster and strengthen that **fidelity.** The couple promise to be faithful to each other until death.

Openness to Fertility. The sharing of love and the transmission of life are essential qualities of marriage. Married love is ordered to the procreation and education of children. A married couple share in the creative power of God. They commit themselves to be open to the gift of children.

The Domestic Church

The first church formed was that of the "house church." In the first days of the Church whole households of believers were welcomed into the Church through Baptism and receiving the good news of salvation in Jesus Christ.

Christian families are the heart of the Church. They are called to be both a sign and a source of God's covenant of love with humankind in Christ. The Second Vatican Council called the family the "ecclesia domestica," or **"domestic church."** The Holy Spirit calls and helps members of Christian families to serve each other and the whole Church in many ways.

Q&A

What needs to be done if a Catholic wants to marry a baptized non–Catholic or a nonbaptized person?
(CCC, 1633–1637)

Such a marriage requires special permission from the Church. The couple needs an express "dispensation" in order to get married.

Differences about religious beliefs and practices, and about marriage can become a source of tension between spouses, especially with regard to passing one's faith on to children.

.... Discuss:

Interreligious marriages are very common in the United States of America. How might you prepare for entering an interreligious marriage? What questions and issues need to be thoroughly discussed before you would enter into a marriage with a non-Catholic or a non-Christian?

Prayer

❖ ❖ ❖

Toward the conclusion of the celebration of Matrimony, the Church asks God's blessings on the newly married couple. Take the time and pray this prayer for married couples you know.

Nuptial Blessing

Let us pray to the Lord for (Name)
and (Name)
who come to God's altar
at the beginning of their married life
so that they may always be united
in their love for each other. . . .
Father, to reveal the plan of your love,
you made the union of husband and wife
an image of the covenant between
you and your people.
In the fulfillment of this sacrament,
the marriage of Christian man and woman
is a sign of the marriage
between Christ and the Church.
Father, stretch out your hand, and bless
(Name) and (Name).
Lord, grant that as they begin to live
this sacrament
they may share with each other
the gifts of your love
and become one in heart and mind
as witnesses to your presence
in their marriage.
Help them to create a home together.

RITE OF MARRIAGE

IMPORTANT TERMS TO KNOW

annulment—the declaration that a marriage was always invalid and a true marriage never existed

divorce—the legal dissolution of a marriage

domestic church—"house church"; the name given to the Christian family; a sign and a source of God's covenant of love with humankind in Christ

fidelity—the keeping of one's marriage promises; an essential quality of a true marriage

indissoluble—a term that applies to a marriage that is concluded and consummated between baptized persons; the marriage is irrevocable and can never be dissolved.

Matrimony—a Sacrament at the Service of Communion that unites a baptized man and woman in a lifelong bond of faithful love as a sign of Christ's love for the Church

CHAPTER SUMMARY

The sacrament of Matrimony calls and consecrates a Christian man and woman to serve the whole Church as a living sign of the unity and love between Christ and the Church. In this chapter we learned:

1. Marriage is part of God's plan of creation. It a covenant by which a man and a woman form an intimate communion of life and love with each other.

2. The sacrament of Matrimony signifies the union of Christ and the Church. The Holy Spirit seals the couple's covenant and expresses the communion of love of Christ and the Church.

3. Marriage is founded on the consent of the spouses. Consent must be given freely and not under constraint. If this consent is lacking, there is no marriage.

4. Since marriage calls and gives the spouses to a public state of life in the Church, it should take place in a liturgical celebration before a witness authorized by the Church (priest or deacon), the witness, and the community of the faithful.

5. Remarriage of validly married spouses who are divorced from living spouses is against the law of God and the Church.

6. Unity, indissolubility, and openness to fertility are essential to marriage.

7. The Christian family is the domestic church where children learn how to pray and serve others according to the example of Christ.

EXPLORING OUR CATHOLIC FAITH

1. Listening to God's Word

Jesus commanded us to love one another as he loves us. Read John 13:31–35. Apply this command of Jesus to marriage. How is it a command that guides spouses to live their covenant of marriage?

2. Understanding the Teachings of the Catholic Church

In the *Constitution on the Church in the Modern World,* the Church teaches that the "well-being of the individual person and of both human and Christian society is closely bound up with the healthy state of conjugal and family life" (47). Using what you have learned in this chapter, explain the meaning of that teaching.

3. Reflecting on Our Catholic Faith

Fidelity between spouses is at the heart of the marriage covenant. Reflect on your life now. In what ways are you a "faithful" person in your current relationships with friends and family? How is that preparing you for the future, perhaps for marriage? Write your reflections in your journal.

4. Living Our Catholic Faith

Review the current commitments you have made. List what you are doing or might do to fully honor those commitments.

Index

A

absolution, 89, 90
Act of Contrition, 90
Advent, liturgical season of, 8–9, 16
altar, 24, 28, 76
altar servers, 23
ambo, 25, 28
ambry, 26, 28
anamnesis, 33, 34, 40
anaphora, 73, 78
annulment, 123, 124
anointing with oil, 26, 28, 51, 59–61, 100
Anointing of the Sick, sacrament of, 92–103
    effects of, 100–101
    institution of, 94–97
    ministers of, 99
    recipients of, 98–99
    rites of, 99–100
    as Sacrament of Healing, 94, 102
Ash Wednesday, 12
assembly, worshiping, 20–23, 71

B

baptism meaning of term, 47, 54
Baptism, sacrament of, 42–55
    effects of, 51–52, 54, 109
    grace of, 51–53
    minister of, 53
    names for, 48
    rite of, 49–51
    Sacred Scripture and, 47–49
    seal of, 51
    unity of Christians and, 53
Baptism of blood, 49
Baptism of desire, 49
baptistry, 25–26, 28
bishop (s)
    ministries of, 21, 63, 99, 110
    ordination of, 112
Blessed Sacrament, 26, 28, 72, 78
blessings, meaning of, 37
breaking of bread, 71, 78

C

candidates, initiation process and, 47
catechesis, sacraments and, 37, 40
catechumen(s), 44, 49
catechumenate, 44, 54
cathedra, 25, 28
chapel of reconciliation, 27
character, sacramental, 36, 51, 61–62, 113
chrism, sacred, anointing with, 51, 59–61, 111
chrism, definition of, 66
chrismation, 60, 66
Christmas, liturgical season, 9–11, 16
church, domestic, 123

church(es), environment of, 18–29
    altar, 24, 28
    ambo, 25, 28
    ambry, 26, 28
    baptistry, 25–26, 28
    cathedra, 25, 28
    chapel of reconciliation, 27, 28
    presider's chair, 25, 28
    stained-glass windows, 25–28
    statues, 25–28
    tabernacle, 26, 28
    tabernacle light, 26, 28
college of bishops, 110, 114
communion. *See* Holy Communion.
compassion, 97, 102
confession, sacrament of, 86. *See also* Penance,
    sacrament of.
confession of sins, 87, 90
Confirmation, sacrament of, 56–67
    definition of, 66
    effects of, 64–65
    minister of, 63
    name for, choosing, 63
    preparation for, 62
    recipients of, 62
    rite of, 59–63
    sponsor for, 62–63
    in Western vs Eastern churches, 60, 63
consecrate, meaning of term, 106, 114
consecratory prayers in Holy Orders, 112–13
consent, matrimonial, 122
contrition, 87, 90
conversion, mystery of, 84–85, 86, 90

D

deacon(s)
    ministries of, 22, 111, 113
    ordination of, 113
diaconate, 111. *See also* deacons; Holy Orders,
    sacrament of.
divorce, 120, 124
domestic church, 123, 124

E

Easter, liturgical season of, 15, 16
Easter Triduum, 12–14, 16
Easter Vigil, 14, 46
epiclesis prayer, 33, 34, 40
    in Anointing of Sick, 100
    in Baptism, 50
    in Confirmation, 61, 64–65
    in Holy Orders, 112–13
episcopate, 110. *See also* bishop(s); Holy Orders,
    sacrament of.
eucharist, meaning of term, 71
Eucharist, sacrament of, 68–79
    as center of Church's life, 70–71
    effects of, 76–77